SIMPLE SOCKS

Priscilla's Sock Song

sung to the folk tune "Shortnin' Bread"

Two little socks, one half-done,
Can't stop knittin' 'cause it's so much fun.
The feet are pink and the heels are green,
If you're walkin' in the dark, you're sure to be seen.

> Mama's little baby loves short-row, short-row,
> Mama's little baby loves short-row heels.

Two little socks, lyin' in bed,
One is yellow and the other one's red.
The doctor said, and I know it's true,
"Short-row toes are good for you!"

> Mama's little baby loves short-row, short-row,
> Mama's little baby loves short-row toes.

Lyrics courtesy of Paulen Moore, Texas

SIMPLE SOCKS
Plain and Fancy

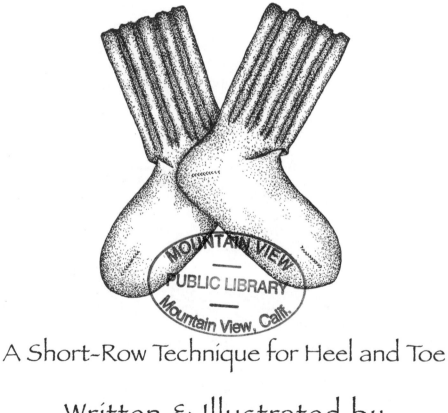

A Short-Row Technique for Heel and Toe

Written & Illustrated by
Priscilla A. Gibson-Roberts

Nomad Press
PO Box 484
Fort Collins, CO 80522-0484

ISBN 0-9668289-4-1 softcover
Library of Congress Card Number 00-105248

*The Library of Congress catalogs the
hardcover edition of this book as follows:*
Gibson-Roberts, Priscilla A.
Simple socks, plain and fancy : a short-row technique
for heel and toe / written & illustrated by
Priscilla A. Gibson-Roberts.
Cedaredge, CO : Nomad Press, c2001.
p.   cm.
ISBN 0-9668289-1-7
1. Knitting. 2. Socks.
I. Title.
TT825 .G72 2001
746.43/20432 21

05 07 09 08 06 04
5 7 9 10 8 6 4

This version of *Simple Socks* is the same in its essentials
as the 2001 hardcover version. The text and images have all
been slightly modified. The layout has been changed.
The charts of average sizes in chapter 1 have been simplified.
The index is entirely new, and more comprehensive.
The city of publication has changed.

Books by Priscilla A. Gibson-Roberts

Knitting in the Old Way:
Designs and Techniques from Ethnic Sweaters
2004

Simple Socks: Plain and Fancy
2001, 2004

High Whorling:
A Spinner's Guide to an Old-World Skill
1998

Ethnic Socks and Stockings:
A Compendium of Eastern Design and Technique
1995

Salish Indian Sweaters:
A Pacific Northwest Tradition
1989

Knitting in the Old Way
1985

"I do believe in simplicity. . . . Simplify the problem of life, distinguish the necessary and the real."

—Henry David Thoreau, 1848

TABLE OF CONTENTS

LIST OF ILLUSTRATIONS

ESSENTIAL REFERENCE INFORMATION

ACKNOWLEDGMENTS

I consider myself to be one of the luckiest people in the world. My family and fiber friends are always ready to lend a hand, often encouraging me to move ahead when I would just as soon quit. As always, Noel Thurner and Nelda Davis were the pushers—these two have no intent to allow me to rest on my laurels. And with this particular endeavor, a small, dedicated group put in their fair share of time making this book happen. First, my daughter and general editor, Kimberly Roberts, who whipped my text into shape—I offer her a special thanks for making it orderly. Next, my friend, technical editor, and general book guru, Deb Robson, who worked hard, above and beyond the call of duty, to keep all the little gremlins at bay so that no errors crop up (we hope)—her commitment to this project was mind-boggling. For the layout and design of the book, I have my old friends, Kate Martinson and Deb Robson, and my new friend, Ann Green, to thank. And after the original printing of this book, my crazy friend Paulen Moore shared the new lyrics that came to her in the company of a traditional folk tune. For this edition, Katie Banks proofed all the revisions, helped us simplify the charts, and made a wonderful and more thorough index. Last but not least, my husband, Jack—not once did he complain about the hit or miss meals, the unmade beds, the extra vacuuming detail, and so on, although he did grumble when I went beyond my physical limitations. Thank you all. I neither would nor could do it alone.

PREFACE

This is a simple book, but not one filled with designs for you to recreate. Instead of patterns, I offer a structure as the canvas on which you can paint your own pictures. It is a simple structure based on a short-row technique for both heel and toe. When the technique is understood, the execution thereof becomes mindless. This allows you to knit plain socks mindlessly (even when brain-dead) or to put your energies into the design of the sock when an elegant accessory is the goal. Or you can adapt any commercially available sock design to accommodate this heel/ toe. And there are special heel/toe effects unique to the structure, including vertical stripes that fold from heel-back to base, toe-top to sole; horizontal stripes that encircle heel and toe; contrasting-color heels that actually look square, both on the foot and off.

Fitting this sock leaves little to guesswork. The basic proportions of the average foot are easily defined with this sock. Furthermore, it is easy to adapt the shape to suit the foot: the heel and/or toe is easily adjusted to fit the pointed or blunt shape as well as the average foot. A simple chart will make it easy for you to find your size in any gauge.

And this book is not limited just to the technicalities of the short-row heel/toe. In addition, the technical aspects are covered for most design variations you can achieve when working circular. These include color-stranding (two- and three-color carries, both left and right), textured designs, lace patterns, motifs, and intarsia— and the effects those design variations have on gauge and elasticity, thereby altering fit.

Because you will be working on a set of five needles, there will be no confusion as to which stitches are worked for the front/instep or back/sole. Never again will you need to reposition the stitches for the heel! This sock structure also allows you to knit from top down or toe up, depending upon your preference. You will be surprised to find this flexibility becomes very important to sock knitting!

INTRODUCTION

Socks have become my knitting life for a number of years as I researched both historical and ethnic pieces from around the world. Always, in the back of my mind, I imagined that I would find the perfect structure, ready and waiting for me to knit. I found several structures that I liked, but none that was perfect. Regretfully, neither life nor socks is perfect. But this did not deter me from reaching my goal. I found a structure which, after I modified and increased the scope of the idea, became my dream sock.

I have never been enamored of the classic Western-style (European/American) sock. The visual aspects of the heel/gusset are not pleasing to me. Although these heels are fairly durable, they are next to impossible to replace. This leaves darning as the principal repair option. And let's face it, even the most careful darning still looks patched. Furthermore, while all the various toe shapings are in fact symmetrical, they do not appear so when on the foot. Granted, the toes of the human foot are not symmetrical, but I prefer a sock that does not emphasize the asymmetrical aspect.

I love Eastern-style (Middle Eastern/Central Asian) socks because they are visually stimulating, with fanciful designs and color combinations. Some have really great toe-shaping, but the best are not the simplest to execute. While the heels of most are pleasant to the eye, they are not particularly durable. They are, however, easy to replace, thus eliminating the need to darn. I love to start at the toe, personally, although I am not fond of picking up the stitches to insert the heel.

It has been a long search to find my dream sock, studying and comparing countless sock structures. Much to my surprise, I found the key when I purchased a pair of designer-label, manufactured socks because I liked the simple lace panels. My thoughts were to decipher and use the panels in my own work. But the sock fit as though created for my foot! At first glance, it appeared to be like countless other commercial socks with the typical, machine-made, short-row shaping. The difference? Unlike most commercial socks, the proportions matched a real foot. It did not depend on the elasticity of knitting to make the sock fit. Instead, this pair was shaped to fit, with a more generous cup at both heel and toe. With my structure now in mind, all that remained was determining what method of short-row shaping resulted in excellence.

Short-row heels have been around since the beginning of knitting, dating back to ancient socks found in Egypt. In most references, this style of heel is referred to as a peasant or hourglass heel. I find it interesting that variations of this heel are found throughout the hand-knitting world: many rudimentary, a few refined. Yet in no culture is this heel used extensively. Its most common form depends upon knitting one stitch less on the end of every row to build the heel-back, one stitch more at the end of every row to create the heel-base. How the back and base are united into a single unit is the significant factor determining whether the result is crude or elegant. I also find it most interesting that I never discovered a short-row toe in hand knitting, and yet this toe is the mainstay of the machine-knitting world.

What is so wonderful about this heel and toe structure for the hand knitter? First, it is easy when the technique is fully understood, appearing magically on the needles. It is durable in its simplest form, equally elastic in all directions to make it contour to the foot. And when heel or toe needs repair, replacement rather than darning is simple, thus eliminating the patched look. Simple adaptations allow for custom fitting to any shape foot. The socks are easy to adorn with the most elaborate patterns without affecting the construction of either heel or toe; in fact, many patterns are easy to continue into both heel and toe. I look at these socks as my sock knitter's nirvana—that state of perfect bliss attained when my knitting is free of all frustration and I am absorbed in the spirit of the process. I hope that you will find the structure equally exciting.

Chapter 1
Sock Sizing

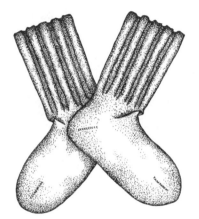

You can be off and running with only two foot measurements!

- **L,** length (see page 18 for how to measure)
- **C,** the circumference of the widest part

Chapter 1 shows you how to measure, how to customize, and how to shape crew and knee socks.

In case you want to knit socks for someone you can't measure, this chapter also includes charts with measurements for average-sized people—from child's small to man's extra-large—at gauges from 5 to 10 stitches per inch.

In order to understand how the short-row sock breaks down into sections, you must understand how it is sized to fit the foot. Looking at length first, you do not need to know the length of the entire foot. Rather, when knitting from the top down, you need to know how long the sock must be prior to commencing the toe shaping. Or should you choose to knit from the toe up, you need the length from the tip of the toe to the point where the heel begins. To measure this length, henceforth designated as L, measure from the tip of the longest toe to the point at the center at the ankle-bone protrusion. I place a ruler on the floor at the inside edge of the foot, with the person seated and the foot resting lightly on the floor. Reduce L slightly so the elasticity of the knit structure will conform closely to the foot.

Several handy rule-of-thumb foot proportions follow from this measurement of L. The length of the foot from the toe to the ankle is the same as the length from the back of the heel to the beginning of the toe shaping. The length of the leg in a typical crew sock is also the same as or slightly more than this measurement.

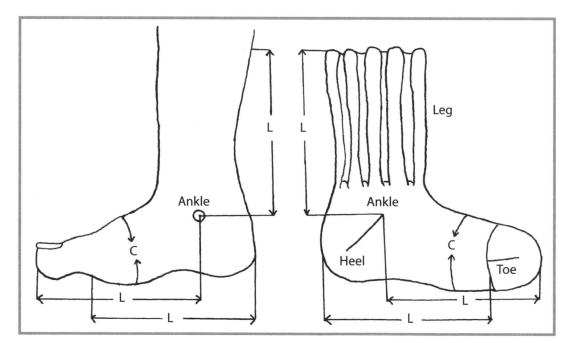

Measuring C & L (circumference and length),
the two important measurements for knitting short-row socks.

The circumference, C, is measured at the widest part of the foot, around the ball. Again, the person must be seated, but now the foot is extended into space. The tape measure must be wrapped securely around the foot, allowing NO ease. For most people, the circumference of the ankle is slightly smaller than the ball-of-foot measurement, but requires no adjustment because this bit of excess improves the fit of the heel.

The circumference in stitches equals gauge multiplied by inches. For those preferring a snug fit, decrease by about 5%; for those preferring a loose fit, increase by 5%. When inches are converted to stitches, the number should be evenly divisible by 4 (when no center stitch is required for design) or by 4 plus or minus 2 (for center-front and center-back stitches); adjust down when possible, unless a pattern repeat requires otherwise.

The leg is the ribbing of a crew sock. The ankle section is the part of the crew sock between the ribbing and the heel shaping. As I like a slightly longer total leg, I knit the ribbing to equal L, then commence with the ankle section. The number of rows necessary for the ankle section can be calculated as 20% of C in stitches; i.e., if C is 60 stitches, there will be 12 rows in the ankle section (60 X 20%).

The ankle and foot of a crew sock are usually worked in stockinette, with one major exception. For either a high arch or flat feet, the elasticity of ribbing (especially a K2-P2 ribbing) allows the sock to contour to the foot more closely. Therefore, for these feet I continue the ribbing down the front of the ankle and foot sections to the toe. I take care to center the ribbing on the front when I begin, starting and ending a K2-P2 ribbing with K1.

To customize fit, the remaining measurement is one of the eye. Look at the person's toe and heel. Are they blunt, average, or pointed (second toe longer than big toe)? By judging what kind of toe/heel is to be fitted, you can determine how many stitches are required between the yarn-overs in the short-row technique that will be described shortly. A very blunt toe/heel will require about 25% of C; an average toe/heel, about 20% of C; a pointed toe/heel, about 15% of C. In every case, this number must be rounded off to the nearest even number when the number of heel/toe stitches (50% of C) is an even number, or to the nearest odd number when the number of heel/toe stitches (50% of C) is an odd number.

To understand this last measurement, you must have a general understanding of how the short rows develop. One less stitch is worked on each row. Then the work is turned and each row commences with a yarn-over. The number of stitches between the next-to-last yarn-over (purl side) and the last yarn-over (knit side) equals 20% of the circumference for an average foot (stitches between yarn-overs: 20% of C).

Basic proportions for a crew sock

Sock circumference: C = 100% of number of stitches necessary

(gauge × inches, the number divisible by 4 for a K2-P2 ribbing)

Number of rows in ankle section: A = 20% of C

Number of heel/toe stitches: 50% of C

Stitches between yarn-overs: 20% of C

(15% for pointed toes or 25% for blunt toes)

Length: As measured, or L = C − 1" (or C = L + 1")

Note: Although calculations may result in slight differences between the number of ankle rows and the number of stitches between yarn-overs, you can use the same number for both in the real world. This way, you only need to remember one number after casting on. I often round the ankle-row number down on children's socks and up on adult sizes; adults tend to need more ankle rows than children do.

With only a measurement of circumference or length, you can guesstimate the other numbers by the average proportions noted above. In the arena of guesstimating, there is another interesting proportion used when I was a child: the distance around a tightly doubled fist equals the total length of the foot. But an accurate measurement is always preferable. For general measurements and guidelines, see pages 23–24.

But as we all know, all socks are not crew socks. And when we get into longer socks, such as knee socks, we have to shape to fit the leg. Knee socks for small children are easiest to fit. Because their legs have not developed distinct contours, all you have to do is work the calf with a size larger needle, returning to the smaller

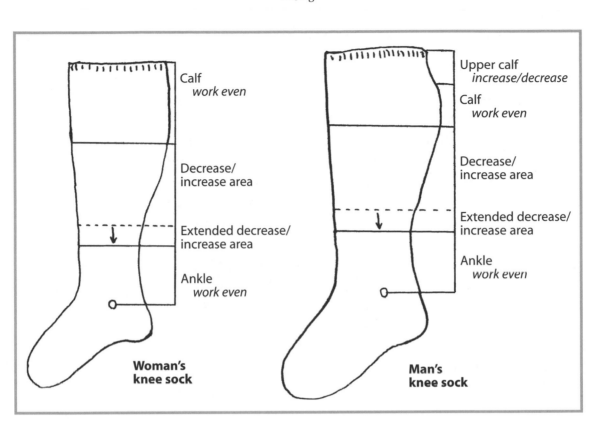

Division of the knee sock into sections for shaping of the leg.

needle for the ribbing (or edging of choice). Shaping knee socks by needle size works equally well for adults, if the instep and leg are worked entirely in a K2-P2 ribbing.

For older children and adults, there are two ways to adjust for the changing girth of the leg: (1) the Eastern way (toe-to-top), with increases hidden in pattern, either randomly or methodically placed, and (2) the Western way (top-to-toe), with decreases outlining and defining a seam up the back. Western knee socks conform more closely to the contours of the leg with the fit holding them in place, whereas Eastern stockings do not conform to the contours of the leg. Instead, they depend upon elasticity for fit, with only limited increase in girth, and often depend upon a tied garter to hold them up. Many Eastern styles allow for a large ankle circumference that needs few increases to fit the upper leg. This shaping has a purpose: when the socks become too warm, they can be pushed down loosely around the ankle, much like the leg warmers that were popular among exercise enthusiasts in the 1980s.

Sizing a Western knee sock to fit the contours of the leg is much simpler than you might think. You will need to measure the circumference of the calf and the length of the leg from the point of the ankle to the top of the sock. To determine the number of decreases, subtract the foot circumference in inches from the leg circumference in inches, and multiply by the gauge. Because the decreases are paired on each side of the back seam stitch/stitches, divide this number by two for the number of decrease rows. If the paired decreases lean away from the seam stitch (decrease leans to the right on the right side, K2tog, and to the left on the left side, SSK), the decreases will make an outstanding line. If the paired decreases lean toward the seam stitch (decrease leans to the left on the right side, SSK, and to the right on the left side, K2tog), the decrease line will be less visible—instead, there will be blips at the point of decrease. These blips were called "full-fashion" marks in the 1950s.

To determine the position of the decrease rows, the length of the leg can be divided roughly into thirds: 1/3 for the calf, 1/3 for the decrease section, 1/3 for the extended ankle. In reality, the decrease section needs to be a bit longer than the other two sections, so I borrow some from the ankle portion. Men's knee socks may need more shaping than women's, because men's calf muscles are often more pronounced. A small reduction in the ribbing, then increasing to the full girth quickly at the top of the calf section accommodates the gender difference. The decreases shaping the calf can be evenly spaced, but I find knee socks fit best when the decreases are more closely spaced in the upper half, more widely spaced in the lower half of the decrease section.

Although Western knee socks are traditionally worked top-down, I prefer to reverse the direction, working toe-up in most cases. Therefore, I pair increases on each side of the center back seam when I am shaping knee socks.

Guidelines for average fit
for different sizes at different gauges

	Gauge in stitches per inch (2.5 cm)					
	5	6	7	8	9	10

Child shoe size 3–7   C = 5½″ (14 cm)   L = 4½″ (11.5 cm)

	5	6	7	8	9	10
Cast-on stitches	28	32	40	44	48	52
Ankle rows	6	6	8	8	10	10
Heel/toe stitches	14	16	20	22	24	26
Stitches between yarn-overs	6	6	8	8	10	10

Child shoe size 8–13   C = 6½″ (16.5 cm)   L = 5½″ (14 cm)

	5	6	7	8	9	10
Cast-on stitches	32	40	44	52	60	64
Ankle rows	6	8	8	10	12	12
Heel/toe stitches	16	20	22	26	30	32
Stitches between yarn-overs	6	8	8	10	12	12

Woman's small   C = 7½″ (19 cm)   L = 6½″ (16.5 cm)

	5	6	7	8	9	10
Cast-on stitches	36	44	52	60	68	72
Ankle rows	8	8	10	12	14	14
Heel/toe stitches	18	22	26	30	34	36
Stitches between yarn-overs	8	8	10	12	14	14

Woman's medium   C = 8″ (20 cm)   L = 7″ (17.7 cm)

	5	6	7	8	9	10
Cast-on stitches	40	48	56	64	72	80
Ankle rows	8	10	12	14	14	16
Heel/toe stitches	20	24	28	32	36	40
Stitches between yarn-overs	8	10	12	14	14	16

C = circumference and L = length (see pages 18–20)

Guidelines for average fit
for different sizes at different gauges

Gauge in stitches per inch (2.5 cm)

Woman's large, man's small C = 8½" (21.5 cm) L = 7½" (19 cm)

	5	6	7	8	9	10
Cast-on stitches	44	52	60	68	76	84
Ankle rows	8	10	12	14	16	16
Heel/toe stitches	22	26	30	34	38	42
Stitches between yarn-overs	8	10	12	14	16	16

Woman's extra large, man's medium C = 9" (23 cm) L = 8" (20 cm)

	5	6	7	8	9	10
Cast-on stitches	48	56	64	72	80	92
Ankle rows	10	12	14	14	16	18
Heel/toe stitches	24	28	32	36	40	46
Stitches between yarn-overs	10	12	14	14	16	18

Man's large C = 9½" (24 cm) L = 8½" (21.5 cm)

	5	6	7	8	9	10
Cast-on stitches	48	56	68	76	84	92
Ankle rows	10	12	14	14	16	18
Heel/toe stitches	24	28	34	38	42	46
Stitches between yarn-overs	10	12	14	14	16	18

Man's extra large C = 10" (25.5 cm) L = 9" (23 cm)

	5	6	7	8	9	10
Cast-on stitches	52	60	72	80	88	100
Ankle rows	10	12	14	16	18	20
Heel/toe stitches	26	30	36	40	44	50
Stitches between yarn-overs	10	12	14	16	18	20

C = circumference and L = length (see pages 18–20)

Chapter 2
Crew Socks

Top-to-Toe and Toe-to-Top

Here's an overview of your fundamental choices when making a sock, including a full description of the short-row technique for shaping the heel and toe. You can use this method to improve any sock pattern!

Most Western sock-knitters work top-to-toe. Most Eastern sock-knitters work toe-to-top. This chapter describes the best techniques for casting on and binding off for each approach, as well as how to divide stitches on the needles, how to place the beginnings of the rounds, and how to handle joins and ends.

General notes on gauge and needles

The gauge calculation for socks determines which needle size and stitch counts will be used for the foot. Everything is calculated from that foundation, and always remember that the tighter the stitches in the foot (short of being boardlike), the more durable the sock. Because I use two sizes of needles, one size for the foot and one size for the upper leg, the primary gauge is calculated for the smaller set of needles.

The stitches for the upper part of the leg must be looser to accommodate the increasing girth and for pulling on the sock. In addition, the cast-on or bind-off edge at the top must be very elastic to withstand repeated stretching when pulling the sock on and off. I work the upper half of the leg ribbing and the cast-on or bind-off on needles one size larger than those I use for the foot.

In the description of working from top-to-toe, you will find recommended cast-on techniques to maximize elasticity. In the description of working from toe-to-top, you will find a bind-off technique with the same purpose.

Regardless of the style or direction of knitting, I always work with a set of five double-point needles. This eliminates the confusion of repositioning the stitches on the needles at the heel. Knitters used to working on sets of four needles will find the additional needle eliminates the problem of a loose stitch where one needle ends and another

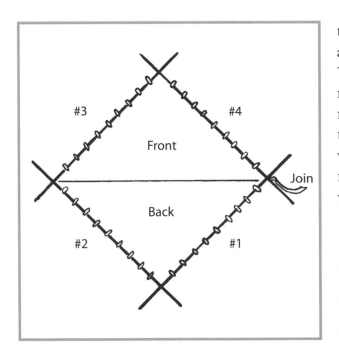

Needle positions with join at the side. For the first sock/left foot, the heel is worked on needles #1 and #2. For the second sock/right foot, the heel is worked on needles #3 and #4.

begins. Why? When knitting with four needles, the work is always under tension in the resulting triangle. With a fifth needle, the work lies in a square with each corner more relaxed. This allows the tension on the corners to remain relatively constant where one needle ends and another begins.

Dividing the stitches

From the beginning and throughout the knitting, the stitches are evenly divided on four needles: two adjoining needles hold the front half of the stitches of the sock, and two the back half. I have been strongly influenced by Eastern sock knitting and prefer to have the joins of the rounds located on the insides of the legs rather than at the back. Working in this manner, on my first sock (for the left foot), the #1 and #2 needles are the back and the #3 and #4 needles are the front. On the second sock (for the right foot), the #3 and #4 needles are the back and the #1 and #2 needles are the front. This requires no shifting of stitches when reaching the heel.

To have the join up the center back of the socks, needles #1 and #4 hold the back stitches while needles #2 and #3 hold the front. This means that there is one row less on one-half of the back when working the heel across needles #1 and #4. This is not a problem in a ribbed or solid crew sock, but if your sock is patterned, the yarn must be broken off (or worked from the other end of the ball to eliminate extra ends to work in), and the heel then begun on the #4 needle.

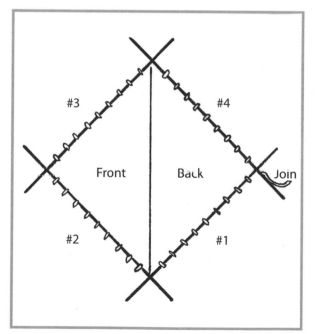

Needle positions with join at the back. Either right or left sock. The heel is worked on needles #1 and #4.

The basics of the short-row technique

In order to understand how the heel is constructed, visualize an hourglass. The upper half of the hourglass is the heel-back; the lower half is the heel-base. (At the toe, these would be toe-top and toe-sole.) How the back and the base are connected to one another varies. I have found that the most durable connection corners the vertical row of stitches around the side. By this, I mean that there is a continuous line of vertical stitches that literally turns a corner where back and base join. Cornering requires the use of yarn-overs and decreasing.

The basics of the short-row technique should be understood prior to working the heel or toe. Shaping results from working one less stitch at the end of each row. Joining the back to the base requires that each row begin with a yarn-over. Therefore, with knit side facing, the stitches are knit up to the last stitch. The work is turned to the purl side, the purl row commencing with a yarn-over.

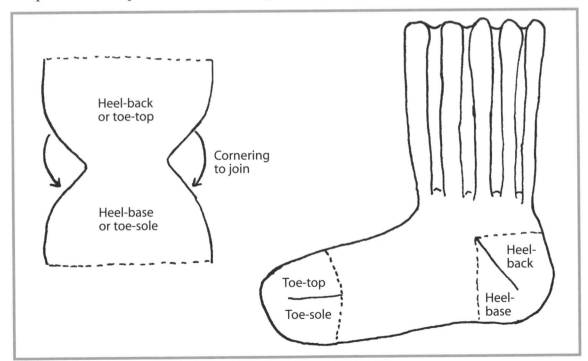

Visualization of hourglass shape inserted into a sock.

If you wrap the purl yarn-over in the standard manner, encircling the entire needle, the resulting loop will be loose and sloppy. This leaves you with a series of lace-like holes marching up the side of the heel. Instead, with purl side facing, take the yarn back under the needle and purl the first stitch. This will mount the yarn-over backwards, i.e., the leading side of the yarn-over loop will be on the back of the needle. But the distance traveled by the yarn will be the same as that of the standard yarn-over on the knit side, thus eliminating any excess. The stitch mount can be corrected to the standard mount prior to working the decrease when working the base of the heel.

The purl row continues to the far side of the heel needles, stopping one stitch before the end. The sock is turned, the knit row then commencing with a yarn-over worked in the standard manner by taking the yarn under the needle to the front and knitting the first stitch.

The work continues in this manner until 20% of the circumference stitches remain unworked between the last yarn-over on the purl side and the last yarn-over on the knit side. At this point, you will be on the knit side, commencing with a yarn-over. The heel back is now completed.

The back and the base are joined as the heel base is worked. Each yarn-over loop on each row on the back of the heel is joined with the next true stitch beyond, using the appropriate decrease (see following page for illustrations of decreases). On the knit side, the joins are made with a K2tog and K3tog (with one exception noted in the step-by-step directions). Before working the Ktogs, correct the stitch mount by slipping the yarn-over to the right needle; then with the left needle tip reverse the stitch mount on each stitch separately. On the purl side, the joins are made with an SSP and SSSP. To work the SSP, slip the yarn-over loop as if to knit, then slip the next true stitch as if to knit. Place these two stitches back on the left needle. With right needle tip, go behind these two stitches, entering them from left to right to purl together. The same holds true for the SSSP, except in this case slip the first yarn-over as to knit, slip the second yarn-over as if to knit, then proceed as with the SSP.

In my socks, the toe is worked the same as the heel.

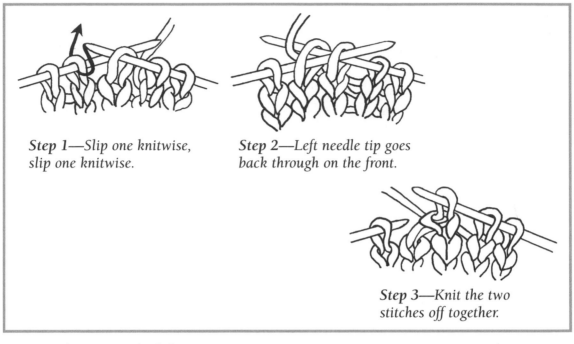

Step 1—*Slip one knitwise, slip one knitwise.*

Step 2—*Left needle tip goes back through on the front.*

Step 3—*Knit the two stitches off together.*

Decrease leaning to the left, SSK version.

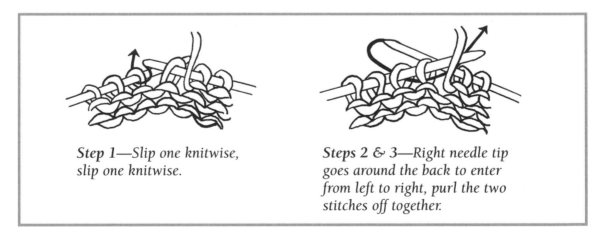

Step 1—*Slip one knitwise, slip one knitwise.*

Steps 2 & 3—*Right needle tip goes around the back to enter from left to right, purl the two stitches off together.*

Decrease leaning to the left, SSP version.

Working top-to-toe

This direction for knitting a sock is most recognizable to the Western knitter. When beginning at the top, the first step is to recognize the importance of the cast-on. It must be very elastic to withstand repeated stretching when pulling the sock on and off. Furthermore, if the cast-on is too snug, the sock will tend to slip down the leg. All of the cast-ons I recommend are long-tail techniques, for maximum elasticity.

Cast on using needles one size larger than those for which you have figured gauge and with which you will work the ankle, heel, foot, and toe of the sock. After you cast on, work half the length of the leg ribbing on the larger needles. Then change to your "regular" needles for the rest of the sock.

Regardless of the cast-on used, all stitches should be cast onto one needle. The stitches can then be divided onto two needles. Lay these two needles straight, then fold the row of stitches in half. Join the circle with the first knit stitch. Redistribute the remaining stitches while

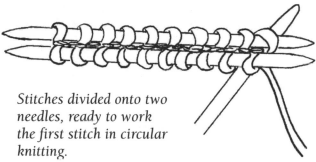

Stitches divided onto two needles, ready to work the first stitch in circular knitting.

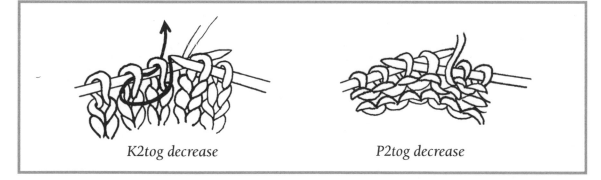

K2tog decrease

P2tog decrease

Decreases leaning to the right.

knitting onto the four needles. Working in this manner will insure that the cast-on is not twisted.

I prefer a K2-P2 ribbing on a crew sock because it is more elastic and thus retains its shape better than a K1-P1 ribbing. For this ribbing, I use a long-tail cast-on often referred to as "the old Norwegian sock cast-on." This cast-on adds an extra twist below each stitch on the needle, thus increasing elasticity over the standard long-tail cast-on. It can be worked in the style typical of the right-hand (English) or left-hand (Continental) carry of the yarn. The simplest manner to execute both follows.

Elastic cast-on, right-hand carry

1   Place a slip knot on the needle for the first stitch, with the long tail yarn coming from the needle around the back and to the front of the left index finger (or thumb). Holding the needle in the right hand, take its needle tip in front of both segments of this yarn, behind both segments, then over the back strand and under the front one. This brings the back yarn to the front and creates a loop on the needle.

2   Continuing to hold the loop under tension on the left index finger, twist the needle slightly up and to the right so it is in knit position.

3   Take the ball yarn in the right hand and wrap it around the right needle tip. This is the normal action for forming a knit stitch in right-hand carry knitting technique.

4   Draw the yarn just wrapped through the loop pulled up from the fingertip. This forms a stitch on the needle.

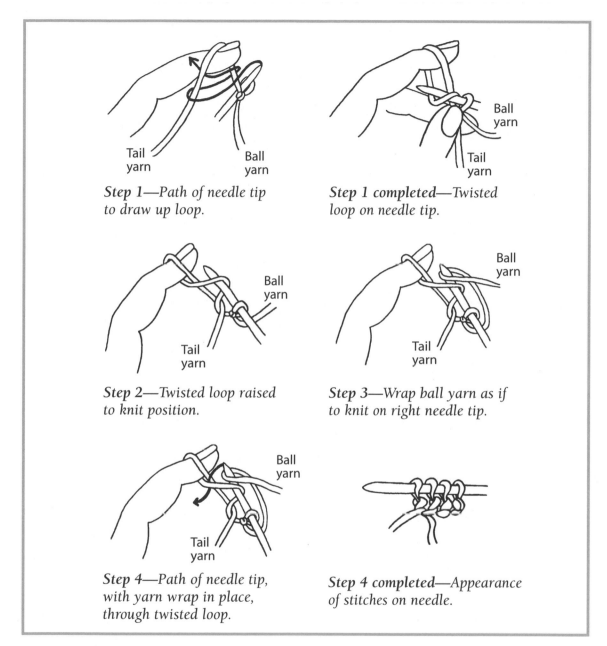

Step 1—Path of needle tip to draw up loop.

Step 1 completed—Twisted loop on needle tip.

Step 2—Twisted loop raised to knit position.

Step 3—Wrap ball yarn as if to knit on right needle tip.

Step 4—Path of needle tip, with yarn wrap in place, through twisted loop.

Step 4 completed—Appearance of stitches on needle.

Elastic cast-on, right-hand carry.

Elastic cast-on, left-hand carry

1 Place a slip knot for the first stitch on the needle, the long tail yarn around the thumb and the ball yarn around the index finger of the left hand, with this first stitch in between.

2 Twist the needle tip in front of the yarn around the thumb, under both yarns on the thumb, pulling the back yarn up on the needle tip to form a loop.

3 Swing the needle over the top of the yarn on the index finger to draw up a loop.

4 Draw this loop down and out to the front to make a stitch on the needle. You may need to turn your thumb slightly to make room for the needle to pass through to the front.

5 Drop yarn from thumb.

6 Pull on the tail yarn with the thumb to secure the loop on the needle.

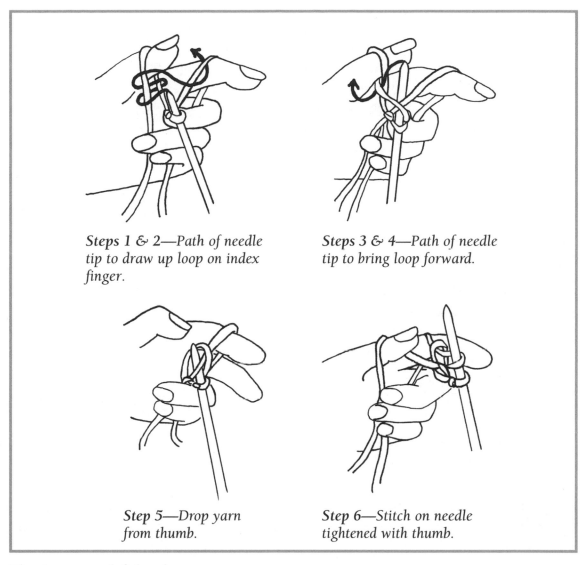

Steps 1 & 2—*Path of needle tip to draw up loop on index finger.*

Steps 3 & 4—*Path of needle tip to bring loop forward.*

Step 5—*Drop yarn from thumb.*

Step 6—*Stitch on needle tightened with thumb.*

Elastic cast-on, left-hand carry.

Knit–purl cast-on

A knit–purl cast-on works well if you plan to use a K1-P1 ribbing or a seed-stitch edging. You will end up with alternating types of loops along your needle, which then become alternating knits and purls in the fabric. You'll cast on with a fluid set of motions, producing two stitches in each complete sequence of movements. The process is lots easier and more rhythmic than it sounds, and the second stitch in each set will feel like it's formed a bit more quickly than the first stitch in the set.

1   Cast on with one needle, held in your right hand. Your left hand holds and controls both strands of yarn, the tail and the one coming off the ball. Make a slip knot in the yarn, leaving a long tail, and unwind about the same amount of yarn from the ball to give yourself working space.

2   Put the slip knot on the needle. It will function as the first purl stitch (you won't see a real purl cast-on stitch until step 4). The back of your left hand is toward you. One strand of yarn (called the finger yarn) goes over your index finger to the back, where it is tensioned in the palm by your second, third, and/or fourth fingers. The other strand (called the thumb yarn) goes down the front of your thumb and to the back, where it is tensioned along with the finger yarn. With tail and ball yarn in left hand, one over the index finger and one over the thumb, begin the cast-on.

3   *Knit-stitch cast-on:* Bring the needle tip forward and down, in front of both yarns, then to the back. Bring it up again between the two yarns, then move it up and over the finger yarn, going to the back to scoop up the yarn. Now the needle tip comes forward, under the thumb yarn, making a circle down behind both yarns on the thumb. As it completes the circle and moves forward and up again, the stitch forms around the needle.

4   *Purl-stitch cast-on:* Take the needle tip to the back and then down behind both yarns, circling the tip toward the front beneath the strands. Take it to the back again between both yarns to bring the thumb yarn behind the finger yarn. With this last move, the stitch forms around the needle.

5 Alternate steps 3 and 4 until you reach the required number of stitches; end with step 3. Because the slip knot at the beginning counts, you will have an even number of stitches.

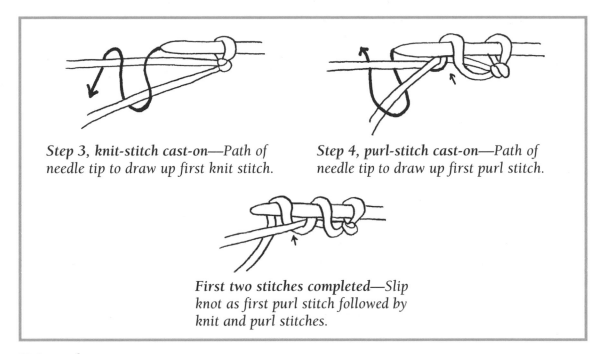

Step 3, knit-stitch cast-on—Path of needle tip to draw up first knit stitch.

Step 4, purl-stitch cast-on—Path of needle tip to draw up first purl stitch.

First two stitches completed—*Slip knot as first purl stitch followed by knit and purl stitches.*

Knit–purl cast-on.

Short-row sock,
beginning at the top and working to the toe

Working with larger needle, cast on the number of stitches required by the size sock desired (C = 100%). Work half of the length of the ribbing on the larger needle size. Then switch to the smaller needle size to complete the ribbing.

Knit the ankle rows in stockinette (ankle rows = 20% of C). The join is positioned on the inside of the leg. The first sock is the left one, so the back of the leg and sole stitches are on needles #1 and #2 (heel/toe stitches = 50% of C).

Work the heel according to the step-by-step instructions on pages 39–42.

Note: The second sock (the right sock) is worked the same as the first until you reach the heel. The heel is worked on the #3 and #4 needles in order to position the join at the inside leg.

Start again here after working the heel:

Knit the foot until the measurement from the outside corner of the heel to the working round equals L. Then commence shaping the toe. The toe is worked exactly the same as the heel.

Two ways for closing the toe will be explained in a moment. For the decorative (zigzag) bind-off, I work the sole of the toe first, then the top. For an invisible finish, I work the top first, then the sole.

At the end of the short-row shaping, the preparation for both techniques is similar. The last row of the toe shaping is worked on the purl side. Turn to the knit side, but do not yarn-over at the start of the row. Arrange the stitches on two needles. Do this by sliding the stitches you just worked for the toe onto one needle. There will be a single yarn-over at the end; adjust its stitch mount. Slide the reserved stitches from the rest of the foot onto the second needle. Hold these two needles together, so the stitches on the toe are closest to you and the working yarn is on the right end of the needles and comes from the stitches on the front needle.

Complete the sock with a zigzag bind-off (page 43) or an invisible finish (pages 44–45).

Step-by-step instructions for the heel

1 Knit across all but the last stitch on the two needles (#1 and #2). Turn.

2 Purl side facing, yarn-over on the working needle by taking the yarn to the back under the working needle to purl the first stitch. Work to one stitch before the end of the second heel needle. Turn.

3 Knit side facing, yarn-over on the working needle by bringing the yarn forward between the needles, then over the working needle to knit the first stitch. Knit to one less stitch than before (up to the paired stitch/yarn-over of the previous row). Turn.

 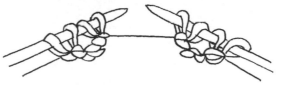

Step 2—Working the first purl stitch, with the yarn-over behind the right needle.

How the stitch loop and yarn-over appear on the purl side.

Yarn-over with *purl* side facing.

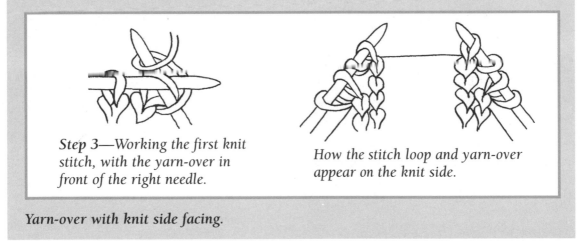

Step 3—Working the first knit stitch, with the yarn-over in front of the right needle.

How the stitch loop and yarn-over appear on the knit side.

Yarn-over with *knit* side facing.

Step-by-step instructions for the heel *(continued)*

Note: The yarn-over loop of the previous row pairs with the first stitch of that row. This makes it easy to determine where to end the row and turn. The yarn-over is also easy to recognize, because a stitch comes up vertically from the row below while the yarn-over loop comes out horizontally from the side of the stitch in the row below. Refer to the illustrations on the previous page.

4   Continue this sequence: yarn-over at the beginning of the row, end row by working one less stitch than before (working up to the paired stitch/yarn-over of the previous row).

5   On an average sock, the back of the heel is complete when 20% of the circumference stitches remain between the yarn-overs. The last turn will bring the knit side facing. Yarn-over and work up to the first available yarn-over at the far side. Adjust the stitch mount by slipping the yarn-over as if to purl to the right needle; enter the slipped yarn-over with the left needle tip from front to back in

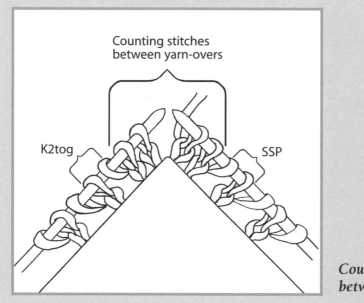

Counting four stitches between yarn-overs.

Step-by-step instructions for the heel *(continued)*

order to reverse the stitch mount, placing it on the left needle. K2tog, joining the yarn-over with the next stitch on the left needle. This will divide the stitch/yarn-over pair, leaving a yarn-over as the next loop on the left needle. Turn.

6   Purl side facing, yarn-over and purl to the first available yarn-over on the next heel needle. Join this yarn-over with the next stitch on the left needle with an SSP as follows. Slip the yarn-over as if to knit, slip the next stitch as if to knit. Place both stitches back on the left needle. Take the right needle tip behind, entering the two loops from left to right. Purl. Turn.

7   Knit side facing, yarn-over and knit to the first available yarn-over on the next heel needle. The next two loops on the left needle are both yarn-overs. Slip both to the right needle singly as if to purl and, with the left needle tip, correct the stitch mount of each individually as it is returned to the left needle. K3tog, joining the two yarn-overs with the next stitch on the left needle. Turn.

8   Purl side facing, yarn-over and purl to the first available yarn-over on the next heel needle. The next two loops on the left needle are yarn-overs. These are joined with the next stitch on the left needle with an SSSP. Slip the first yarn-over as if to knit, slip the second yarn-over as if to knit, slip the next stitch as if to knit. Put all three loops back on the left needle singly. Take the right needle tip behind all three to enter them from left to right. Purl three off together. Turn.

9   Continue in this manner until all the yarn-overs of the heel-back have been consumed in the decrease of the heel-base. The last stitch on each side will consume two yarn-overs. Each turn will also require one yarn-over. Thus, there will be a single yarn-over at the end of each of the two heel needles. On the last turn, the knit side will be facing.

Yarn-over and knit across the heel needles to the yarn-over ending the second heel needle. Move this yarn-over to the next (instep) needle. Begin that

Step-by-step instructions for the heel *(continued)*

needle with a K2tog decrease that joins the yarn-over with the first stitch. Work across the instep needles to the last stitch on the second instep needle. Place the yarn-over on the next heel needle onto the instep needle and join the final instep stitch with this yarn-over using an SSK decrease. Be sure that you have the proper stitch mounts on both of the decreases. Heel is now complete.

The final decrease on the heel may appear to gape, the stitches having loosened while you were working the heel. To avoid leaving a gap, work the decrease and instep stitches of this row onto the heel needle rather than dividing as usual at this point. Then, if necessary, even the tension of the stitches with the tip of the free needle. Divide the stitches as before when knitting the next round. Or close the gap by picking up one stitch in the gap and placing it onto the left needle, then SSSK.

Continue with sock instructions on page 38.

Zigzag bind-off

Here's how to join the toe to the foot with a zigzag bind-off (a technique borrowed from historic Greek socks). Purl one on the back needle and then knit one on the front needle. Pass the first stitch over. Purl on back; pass that stitch over. Knit on front; pass that stitch over. Work across all stitches in this manner. At the end, work the yarn-over with the adjoining stitch. Break off and draw the tail through the last loop to secure the end, and finish the end by weaving it in.

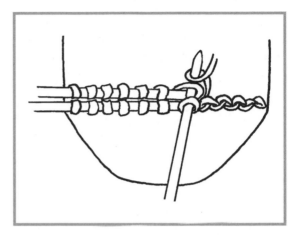

Zigzag bind-off at toe.

Invisible join

If you prefer an invisible join, graft the two groups of stitches together. I prefer to place this graft on the sole, where any irregularity in grafting tension will be hidden. Again, the yarn comes from the right-hand stitch on the front needle. Break off, leaving tail with sufficient length to work across sock. Thread tail into tapestry needle.

Grafting stitches for invisible join:

1   Enter the first stitch on the back as if to knit, but do not remove. Come to the front and enter the first stitch as if to purl, but do not remove.

2   On the back, purl off the first stitch and enter the second as if to knit but do not remove.

3   On the front, knit off the first stitch and enter the second as if to purl but do not remove.

4   Repeat steps 2 and 3 until all stitches have been consumed, taking care to include the final yarn-over with the stitch.

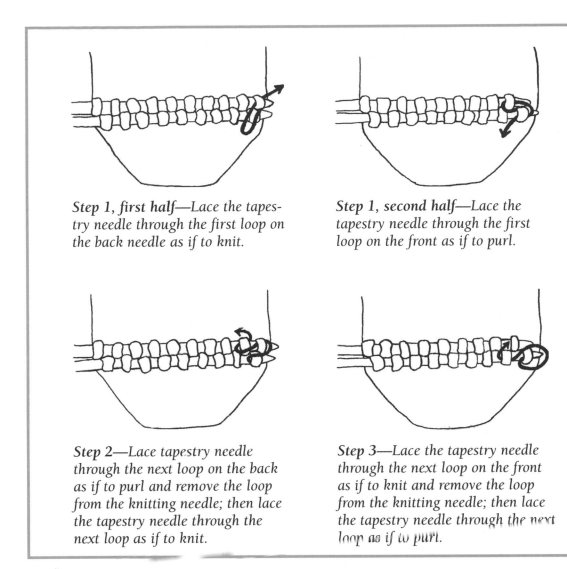

Step 1, first half—*Lace the tapestry needle through the first loop on the back needle as if to knit.*

Step 1, second half—*Lace the tapestry needle through the first loop on the front as if to purl.*

Step 2—*Lace tapestry needle through the next loop on the back as if to purl and remove the loop from the knitting needle; then lace the tapestry needle through the next loop as if to knit.*

Step 3—*Lace the tapestry needle through the next loop on the front as if to knit and remove the loop from the knitting needle; then lace the tapestry needle through the next loop as if to purl.*

Grafting stitches at the toe.

45

Working toe-to-top

To knit socks from the toe up, the Eastern way, is not familiar to many knitters. But once they try it, many become committed. You will want to knit the foot and lower half of the ribbing with a needle small enough to give a very firm gauge, for durability. The upper half of the ribbing should be worked on one size larger needle to increase elasticity for the increasing girth of the leg and to make pulling the sock on and off easy.

To work from the toe up requires an invisible cast-on.

Invisible cast-on

You will need a smooth, slick waste yarn for this. I use a braided nylon cord (called "ravel cord") used for similar purposes by machine knitters. Tie the cord and the sock yarn together with an overhand knot. Do not pull the knot tight, because you will need to remove it when the toe is finished. Using the smaller set of needles, cast on the required number of stitches (50% of C).

1   With a needle in your right hand, position the knot on the needle so the sock yarn comes over the top of the needle and the waste yarn is behind it.

2   Tension the waste yarn on your index finger, with the sock yarn over the thumb on your left hand. Pivot the needle behind the waste yarn to pick up a loop with the sock yarn.

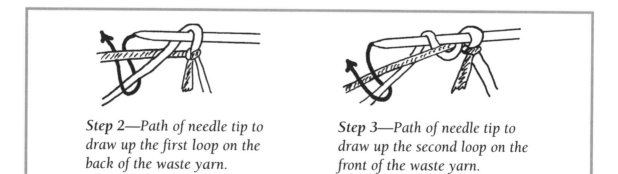

Step 2—Path of needle tip to draw up the first loop on the back of the waste yarn.

Step 3—Path of needle tip to draw up the second loop on the front of the waste yarn.

Invisible cast-on for toe.

3 Pivot the needle to the front of the waste yarn to pick up a loop with the sock yarn.

Continue in this manner until half of the circumference stitches have been mounted on the needle. You will have an equal number of stitches on the cord. (Heel/toe stitches = 50% of C.)

4 At the end, turn, securely tucking the waste yarn over the sock yarn to hold it in position until the first stitch is knitted. The stitches on the needle are those on which the toe is shaped; the stitches on the waste yarn will take the completed toe into the round for the foot of the sock.

Work the toe according to the step-by-step instructions on pages 48–51.

Start again here after working the toe:

After completing the toe, knit the foot until its measurement from the tip of the toe to the working point equals L. Then shape the heel. The heel is worked exactly the same as the toe, working the base of the heel first, then the back. In order to keep the join of the round on the inside of the leg, I knit the heel of the first sock on needles #1 and #2 (the left sock), and that of the second sock on needles #3 and #4 (the right sock).

The final decrease may appear to gape, the stitches having loosened while you worked the heel. To avoid leaving a gap, work the decrease and instep stitches of this row onto the heel needle rather than dividing as usual at this point. Then, if necessary, even the tension of the stitches with the tip of the free needle. Divide the stitches as before when knitting the next round. Or close the gap by picking up one stitch in the gap and placing it onto the left needle, then SSSK.

You are now ready to knit the ankle stitches (ankle rows = 20% of C). When the ankle stitches are complete, begin the ribbing. I use a K2-P2 ribbing because it is more elastic and retains its shape better than a K1-P1 ribbing. Work half the length of the ribbing on the smaller needles used for the foot, then change to the one-size-larger set for the remaining half of the ribbing.

When you reach the length desired, do not bind off. Instead, graft off. (*See instructions on pages 51–53.*)

Step-by-step instructions for the toe

1   Knit across all but the last stitch on the two needles (#1 and #2). Turn.

2   Purl side facing, yarn-over on the working needle by taking the yarn to the back under the working needle to purl the first stitch. Work to one stitch before the end of the second heel needle. Turn.

3   Knit side facing, yarn-over on the working needle by bringing the yarn forward between the needles, then over the working needle to knit the first stitch. Knit to one less stitch than before (up to the paired stitch/yarn-over of the previous row). Turn.

Step 2—Working the first purl stitch, with the yarn-over behind the right needle.

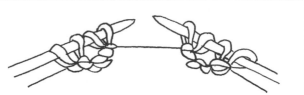

How the stitch loop and yarn-over appear on the purl side.

Yarn-over with purl side facing.

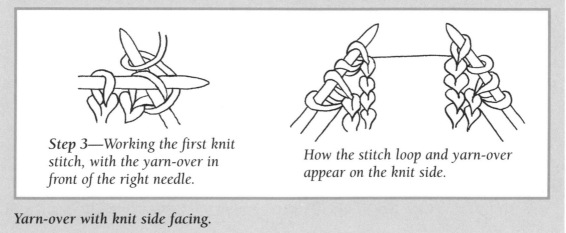

Step 3—Working the first knit stitch, with the yarn-over in front of the right needle.

How the stitch loop and yarn-over appear on the knit side.

Yarn-over with knit side facing.

Step-by-step instructions for the toe *(continued)*

Note: The yarn-over loop of the previous row pairs with the first stitch of that row. This makes it easy to determine where to end the row and turn. The yarn-over is also easy to recognize, because a stitch comes up vertically from the row below while the yarn-over loop comes out horizontally from the side of the stitch in the row below. Refer to the illustrations on the previous page.

4   Continue this sequence: yarn-over at the beginning of the row, end row by working one less stitch than before (working up to the paired stitch/yarn-over of the previous row).

5   On an average sock, the tip of the toe is complete when 20% of the circumference stitches remain between the yarn-overs. The last turn will bring the knit side facing. Yarn-over and work up to the first available yarn-over. Adjust the stitch mount by slipping it as if to purl to the right needle; enter slipped yarn-over with left needle tip from front to back in order to reverse the stitch mount, placing it on the left needle. This will divide the stitch/yarn-over pair, leaving a yarn-over as the next loop on the left needle. Turn.

K2tog— see p. 41

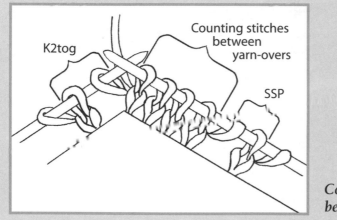

Counting four stitches between yarn-overs.

Step-by-step instructions for the toe *(continued)*

6   Purl side facing, yarn-over and purl to the first available yarn-over on the next toe needle. Join this yarn-over with the next stitch on the left needle with an SSP as follows. Slip the yarn-over as if to knit, slip the next stitch as if to knit. Place both stitches back on the left needle. Take the right needle tip behind, entering the two loops from left to right. Purl. Turn.

7   Knit side facing, yarn-over and knit to the first available yarn-over on the next toe needle. The next two loops on the left needle are both yarn-overs. Slip both to the right needle singly as if to purl and, with the left needle tip, correct the stitch mount of each individually as it is returned to the left needle. K3tog, joining the two yarn-overs with the next stitch on the left needle. Turn.

8   Purl side facing, yarn-over and purl to the first available yarn-over on the next toe needle. The next two loops on the left needle are yarn-overs. These are joined with the next stitch on the left needle with an SSSP. Slip the first yarn-over as if to knit, slip the second yarn-over as if to knit, slip the next stitch as if to knit. Put all three loops back on the left needle singly. Take the right needle tip behind all three stitches and enter them from left to right. Purl three off together. Turn.

9   About halfway through the second half of the toe, you will find making the decreases becomes more difficult because the toe has become somewhat circular. At this point, you will need to divide your work evenly onto two needles (#1 and #2 needles), using a third needle for the working needle.

10   Continue in this manner until all the yarn-overs of the toe-top have been consumed in the decreases. The last stitch on each side will consume two yarn-overs. Each turn will also require one yarn-over. Thus, there will be a single yarn-over at the end of each of the two toe needles. On the last turn, the knit side will be facing. Yarn-over and knit across needle #1. You are now ready to place the waste yarn stitches on a needle. As you do so, note that every

---

Step-by-step instructions for the toe *(continued)*

other stitch on the waste yarn is not in the standard stitch mount and must be adjusted when worked. Divide these stitches on two needles, #3 and #4. On needle #2, work up to the yarn-over. Place this yarn-over onto needle #3, and join the two with a K2tog decrease. Work across needles #3 and #4 to the last stitch on needle #4. Place the yarn-over on needle #1 onto needle #4, and join the two with an SSK decrease. Be sure that you have the proper stitch mounts on both of the decreases. The toe is now complete and you are working in the round on four needles.

Continue working sock with the instructions at the location marked on page 47.

Graft off at top

The graft-off edge is an invisible finish that is significantly more elastic than the standard bind-off. The knit stitches are grafted to the purl stitches in the standard manner, although the result is an invisible edge-finish instead of an invisible join.

Both K1-P1 ribbing and K2-P2 ribbing are grafted off in the same manner. You might note an insignificant distortion of the stitches of the K2-P2, because the yarn must be stretched across the back of two stitches when it passes from front to back, back to front.

Break off a sufficient length to work a full round on the sock, plus some extra for insurance. Thread the yarn into a blunt tapestry needle. *(Illustrations appear on page 52.)*

1   Begin work with the first half of the stitches to be grafted off. Prepare by sliding the knit stitches onto one needle (to lie in the front) and the purl stitches onto another needle (to lie in the back).

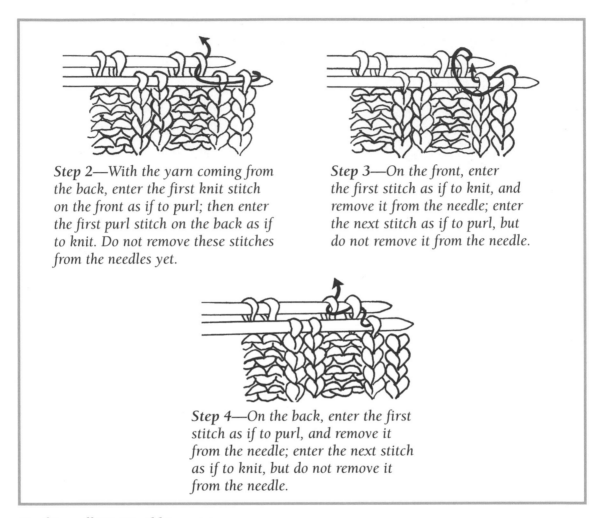

Step 2—With the yarn coming from the back, enter the first knit stitch on the front as if to purl; then enter the first purl stitch on the back as if to knit. Do not remove these stitches from the needles yet.

Step 3—On the front, enter the first stitch as if to knit, and remove it from the needle; enter the next stitch as if to purl, but do not remove it from the needle.

Step 4—On the back, enter the first stitch as if to purl, and remove it from the needle; enter the next stitch as if to knit, but do not remove it from the needle.

Grafting off K2-P2 ribbing at top.

2 With the yarn coming from the back, enter the first knit stitch on the front as if to purl, but do not remove it from the needle. Enter the first purl stitch on the back as if to knit, but do not remove it from the needle.

3 On the front, enter the first knit stitch as if to knit and remove it from the needle; enter the next knit stitch as if to purl, but do not remove it from the needle.

4   On the back, enter the first purl stitch as if to purl and remove it from the needle; enter the next purl stitch as if to knit, but do not remove it from the needle.

Repeat steps 3 and 4 until most of the stitches in the first half have been removed. Slide the remainder of the stitches onto the two needles as before, with the knit stitches on the front needle and the purl stitches on the back needle, and continue grafting off. When one stitch remains on the front needle and one on the back needle, knit off the front stitch and purl off the back stitch. End by entering the first knit stitch removed as if to purl, then take the yarn to the back to work the tail down a rib.

With practice, you may not find it necessary to realign the stitches onto two needles, one for the front stitches and one for the back stitches. I continue to work in this manner because I can lay my work down when necessary without losing track of where I am in the procedure. In order to keep the join of the round on the inside of the leg, I knit the first heel on needles #1 and #2 (the left sock), the second on needles #3 and #4 (the right sock).

Joins and ends

Within a solid section of the sock, I will usually splice the yarn. I break off each ply to a different length on each yarn. The tapered ends are laid together and lightly twisted. If working with a singles yarn, taper the ends and overlap. You will want a splicing length sufficient to knit several stitches with the ends of both yarns.

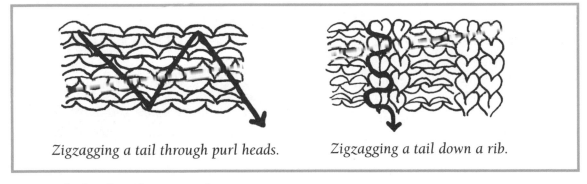

Zigzagging a tail through purl heads.   *Zigzagging a tail down a rib.*

Two methods of working in ends.

53

To work ends in, use a sharp-pointed crewel needle. I do not "weave" the ends in. Instead, I zigzag up and down several times, piercing the backs of the stitches. In the ribbing, I zigzag down a vertical knit row, piercing the stitches.

Other alternatives

When you are shaping the heel and toe, you can work across all the stitches of the back, turning at the end of the needle, instead of working up to the last stitch and turning just before it. On the second row, also work to the end of the heel/toe stitches before turning. Then proceed as usual. This adds two additional rows of depth to the cup of the heel/toe. If you work in this manner, you will have two yarn-overs at each end when you return to knitting in the round. Thus, you must decrease with a K3tog and SSSK as you go into the round.

Those who prefer to work both the ankle and the leg portions in stockinette must make some adjustments, because stockinette is less elastic than ribbing. As before, the lower portion of the leg is knitted on the smaller needles and the upper portion on the larger needles. But the total length of the ankle and leg, including a short ribbing at the top, must not exceed L. Any additional length requires an increase of about 5% in C to accommodate increasing girth. These increases should be placed about midway (or slightly above the midpoint) in the section worked on

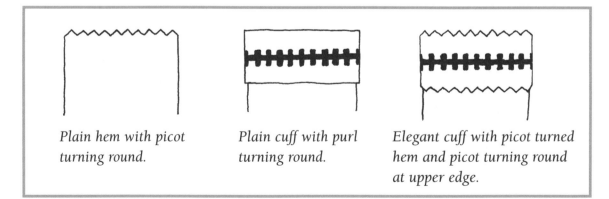

Plain hem with picot turning round.   *Plain cuff with purl turning round.*   *Elegant cuff with picot turned hem and picot turning round at upper edge.*

Hems and cuffs.

54

the larger needles and evenly spaced around the sock. The small section of ribbing at the top should be worked on the smaller needles, thereby equalizing the elasticity of the stockinette and the ribbing.

Not all crew socks have ribbings. Some start with a hem. When I use a hem, I begin at the top, casting onto the smaller-sized needle with an invisible cast-on. When the underside of the hem has been worked on the smaller needles, I change to the larger needle for a turning round. The turning round can be one round of K2tog/yarn-overs, to make a decorative picot edge, or one purl round, for a plain edge. I knit an equal distance, usually one or two rounds less than the underside of the hem. I put the stitches from the cast-on onto the smaller needles, folding the hem into position. The hem is joined to the front by knitting through both the outside stitches and the underside hem stitches.

Cuffs are another option. The outer portion of the cuff is worked on the larger needles, the under portion in ribbing on the smaller needles. The simplest cuffs are ribbing or seed stitch, folded down. Because both of these stitch patterns are reversible, the remainder of the sock can be knitted with no further provision for the cuff.

More decorative cuffs must begin with two or three rounds of an edging that is resistant to rolling; then the decorative pattern can begin. I like the symmetry that comes from repeating the edging at the top of the cuff, just before the ribbing begins. For an elegant cuff, knit a hem with a picot turning round, repeating the picot round for the fold line of the cuff.

When the patterned cuff is completed, turn the knitting *inside out,* reversing the direction you are knitting—otherwise, the cuff will be wrong-side-out when folded over the finished sock. To eliminate a small hole at the point of reversal, yarn-over at the beginning of the round; end the round with an SSK to join the last stitch and the yarn-over.

Comparing top-to-toe and toe-to-top

Top-to-toe socks are often considered superior, because a cast-on at the top is usually more elastic than a standard bind-off. But the graft-off technique used at the top is equally elastic, nullifying this advantage of starting at the top (see pages 51–53).

Suppose you have a given supply of yarn, often the case with handspinners, and you want to use it in a pair of socks. Starting at the top locks you into guesswork. But starting at the toe allows for the equal division of the yarn, knitting to fit the foot and then going as far as the yarn allows (or, if you are lucky, until the desired length is reached).

It is easier to use an invisible cast-on at the toe than to graft the width of the foot, when a smooth toe join is more desirable than the zigzag bind-off of the top-to-toe sock. In some cases, the zigzag bind-off, decorative in itself, can clash with the overall sock design. And people with really sensitive feet may not like the resulting ridge.

For me, it is important when designing to maintain the orientation of the Vs of the knit stitches. So I start at the toe, instead of inverting the V (standing it on its head). This admittedly is a fine point, but one that is important to me—even when I am working at 12 stitches to the inch and no one can see the stitches!

But when it comes time to replace the toe, or the whole foot for that matter, having knitted your socks from the top has advantages. You can just pull the yarn and watch the stitches go. If you have started at the toe, you will have to pick out the stitches of a full round to separate the pieces, then pick up the stitches and work down.

All things considered, the choice of whether to begin at the top or at the toe boils down to personal preference (or limited yarn supply). Having worked extensively from the toe up, I tend to prefer it—most of the time.

Chapter 3
Design

Inspirations and Considerations

Some of these design techniques require short-row shaping:
- Colorful heels and toes
- Games to play with stripes

Others can be applied to any sock structure:
- Color-stranded patterning
- Intarsia motifs
- Abundant textures

Now that you can make basic crew socks with the short-row technique, you will want to consider incorporating design elements. First, be aware that this heel/toe structure can be plugged into any commercial pattern that strikes your fancy. Also, there are variations exclusive to the short-row technique that I will detail for you. For the traditional design techniques, coverage is limited to my methods for working color patterns, texture patterns, and lace patterns, and/or the effects these patterns have upon sock knitting. I leave the designs for you to create, with only one word of caution: do not depend on changing needle sizes to accommodate fit when you incorporate designs. In many cases, you must use increases/decreases to shape the socks, whether they are shorter crew socks or longer knee socks.

For fancy short to mid-length socks, I use the Eastern technique with increases/decreases hidden in the pattern. For fancy crew socks, I place the first increase/decrease row where I normally change needle size for plain crew socks. For patterned knee socks, I use the Western method, with increases/decreases outlining a center-back seam. When you start at the toe, shape with increases; when you start at the top, shape with decreases.

I prefer the "make-one raised" increase (M1R). To execute an M1R, raise the bar between the stitches with the right needle tip and place it on the left needle tip. The bar loop is then knitted so that it is twisted. The direction of the twist will determine whether the increase leans to the left or the right. For a left-leaning loop, lift the bar from back to front; when the loop is placed on the left needle, its leading side will be on the front of the needle and the stitch will twist to the left when knitted through the back. For a right-leaning increase, lift the bar from front to back; when the loop is placed on the left needle, its leading side of the loop will be on the back and the stitch will twist to the right when knitted through the front. When hidden in the pattern, the directionality of the increases is unimportant, but when paired to outline a seam, the increases should lean right on the right side and left on the left side.

For decreases, I use the K2tog and SSK described earlier. I use the K2tog to the right of the seam, the second stitch consuming the first so that the decrease leans to the right. I use the SSK to the left of the seam, the first stitch consuming the second so that the decrease leans to the left.

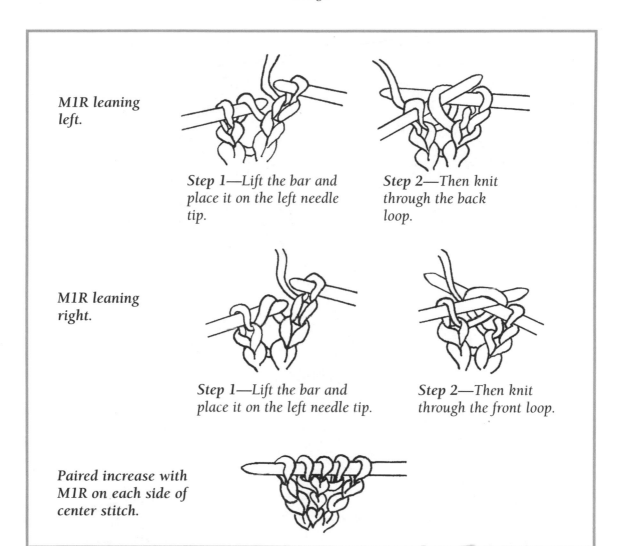

M1R leaning left.

Step 1—*Lift the bar and place it on the left needle tip.*

Step 2—*Then knit through the back loop.*

M1R leaning right.

Step 1—*Lift the bar and place it on the left needle tip.*

Step 2—*Then knit through the front loop.*

Paired increase with M1R on each side of center stitch.

Increase: make-one raised (M1R).

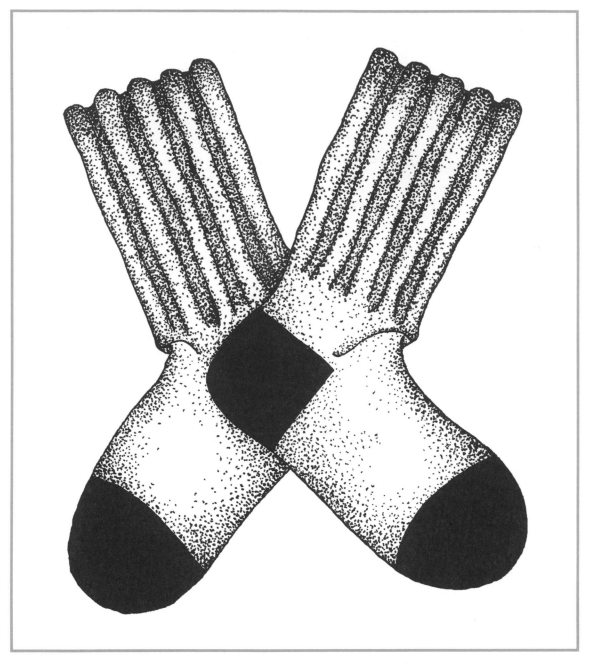

Socks with contrasting color at heel and toe.

Simple elegance
exclusive to the short-row technique

Contrasting color at heel and toe

I have always loved the old-fashioned, manufactured gray boot socks with red heels and toes, the kind that were used to make stuffed monkeys fifty-plus years ago. You cannot get that look with the traditional Western-style hand-knitted sock. But the short-row sock makes the perfect contrasting heel/toe. It's a simple variation that pleases my senses.

When I make the contrasting heel, on the first two rows I work all the way across the heel stitches (50% of C) in the new color, instead of working up to but not including the last stitch of the row. This makes the heel consume a full half of the circumference, adding some depth to the heel cup. On the last row, there will be two yarn-overs at each end to decrease into the join. When going back into the round, you will work across the heel stitches in the main color, consuming the yarn-overs at the end with an instep stitch in a K3tog. Continuing across the instep stitches, you will consume the yarn-overs at the end with an instep stitch, using an SSSK. To maintain balance, I work the toe in the same manner.

Horizontal stripes with bull's-eye effect at heel and toe

Another simple design is horizontal stripes. I usually work these on the heel/toe of a totally striped sock. When changing colors at the heel/toe, I yarn-over in the new color, twist the new yarn with the dropped yarn, then begin knitting the stripe.

I work an even number of rows in the stripes to keep the color changes all on the same side of the heel/toe. Working with an even number of rows also allows me to split a stripe around the heel, working half of the stripe before the heel and half of the stripe when I start the heel. I then complete half of the stripe as I finish the heel and the remaining half after the heel. For example, when working a four-row stripe, I begin to work on the heel in the middle of the stripe sequence (after two rows). Two rows complete the stripe at the beginning of the heel and two rows begin a new stripe at the completion of the heel. With the heel completed, working in the

Socks with horizontal stripes extending into heel and toe.

round again, two rows finish the stripe. Because the stripes are worked back and forth across the heel-back and the heel-base, they encircle the heel, like the center of a target.

Smoothing out joins on stripes

There will be a jog in the stripe on the opposite side of the join. In finer yarns, the jog is essentially not a problem. It exists, but at such a small scale that an optical illusion takes over and the stripes around the heel appear to be smoothly continuous. When working with heavier yarns, the jog at the beginning of the round can be distracting in the main body of the sock, as well as on the heel/toe. To disguise the jog at the color change in the main body of the sock, I use a technique found in traditional Danish knitting. Knit the first stitch of each new stripe with both colors. Continue knitting around, completing the first row of the new stripe and the first stitch of the next round (knit with both colors of the former round). Now, pull the strand of yarn that has been dropped. It will hide beneath the new color and the jog in the stripe will magically disappear.

Minimizing the jog on the heel/toe is not quite as simple. At a gauge of six or fewer stitches to the inch, the transitional jogs and the slight color-shifts at the decreases may offend some knitters' sensibilities. Up to this point, the descending side of the heel/toe is a mirror image of the ascending side. You can improve the illusion of stripe continuity by shifting the row on which you reverse directions in the sequence.

The last knit row becomes the center of the bull's-eye. The beginning of the round is shifted to the opposite side of the heel/toe; therefore you must break off or weave the yarn not in use across the back of this row. The first row of the descending side will be a purl row, worked in the color that matches the last purl row on the ascending side. Continue to knit the row-stripe sequence in the reverse order of the first side of the heel/toe. On the final knit row, the last knit stitch will consume the two yarn-overs with a K3tog. If you are to continue the beginning of the round as established on the main body of the sock, you must now break off both colors and return to the far side, unless you are in the middle of a stripe. You will now work in the round across the next two needles, up to but not including the last stitch. This last stitch will consume the two yarn-overs on the next needle with an SSSK.

Summarizing the process, the ascending side begins on a knit row and ends on a purl row. The next knit row is a dividing row between the ascending and descending sides. It is the center of the bull's-eye; there will always be an odd number of rows in the bull's-eye. The descending side begins on a purl row and ends on a knit row. Beginning with the first purl row, the row-color sequence is worked as a mirror image of the first side (excluding the center row of the bull's-eye). Return to working in the round when the sequence is completed.

This technique is not perfect, but it is the only solution I could find to deal with the jog. Unless something better comes along, perhaps the best solution is to confine the use of horizontal stripes to finer yarns.

Fancier stripes, or color-stranded patterns

And yes, you can color-strand simple repeats around the heel/toe. I suggest that you center them, instead of carrying them all the way to the edges. Then you do not have to deal with an extra yarn in the yarn-over decrease at the end of each row.

Vertical stripes that fold around heel and toe

For me, the most exciting design possibility exclusive to the short-row technique is vertical stripes that fold around heel and toe from the back to the base, the top to the sole. Because the vertical line of knit stitches corners at the join, the stripes also corner at the sides of both heel and toe, producing continuous stripes.

To center the stripes, there must be odd numbers of stitches on both the front and back needles. Plan for these stripes when you cast on, using a stitch count for C that is divisible by 2 but not by 4 (for example, 50 or 70). I prefer to work these stripes across the full width of the heel/toe, working to and including the last stitch before turning, as described above (page 61, "Contrasting color"). I work a two-row horizontal stripe in the contrasting color, across and back on the heel (twice around on the toe). Then I work the vertical stripes, alternating between the main color and the contrasting color.

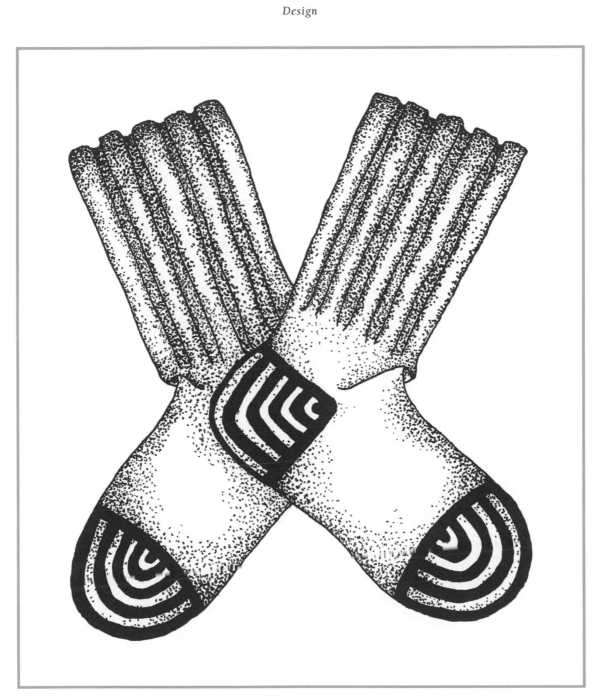

Socks with vertical stripes folding around heel and toe.

Socks with vertical stripes, top-to-toe.

You do not have to do anything special to make this work—and it looks more complicated than it is. When you are ready to insert the first stripe, yarn-over with the tail of the main color and knit the first stitch in the main color. Twist the contrasting-color and main-color yarns, then knit the next stitch in the contrasting color. The remaining stitches are worked in the alternating colors. And, at the beginning of each row, yarn-over with the yarn of the first stitch. These yarn-overs are consumed by a stitch of the opposite color on the decrease half of the heel.

The heel and toe will have double-thick fabric, increasing both comfort and durability. Because this technique can produce very tight stitches at the heel and toe, I knit these sections on needles one size larger than those I use for the plain stockinette sections. When starting at the the toe, the cast-on is in the contrasting color.

Used alone, the vertical stripes at heel and toe make a plain sock special, especially when it will be worn with sandals. But when used in combination with other patterns, this heel/toe variation becomes a smashing design element!

Vertical stripes on the entire sock

You can make the entire sock in vertical stripes. The stripes begin on the front, go down the instep, travel around the toe from top to bottom, then continue up the sole, through the heel, and on up the back of the leg—broken only by the join! Side stripes come down to corner at the heel, proceed to the toe, corner again, and go right back up the same side.

For this to happen, the front and back of the sock must be mirror images, beginning and ending with the same color. Therefore, the center side stripe will double back on itself, creating a double-width stripe at each side.

I start these socks at the top with a standard long-tail cast-on (not the old Norwegian sock cast-on), using a double yarn in one color. No ribbing: just work one round of purl with the double yarn, then go right into the stripes. When shaping the heel/toe, work across all the heel/toe stitches and turn (see page 61, "Contrasting color"). When changing colors, remember to yarn-over with the yarn of the first knit stitch, knit the stitch, twist the two yarns, then knit the second stitch in the alternating color. Match the zigzag bind-off with the cast-on color.

Socks with Eastern ethnic flair, pattern outlined with borders at front, back, and sole.

When you knit a whole sock in stripes, work on needles one size larger than you would ordinarily use for that particular yarn, because vertical stripes are not very elastic. The upper leg must be worked on needles yet another size larger.

Combining the best of two worlds

When knitted from toe-to-top, this structure is ideal for knitting socks that have the often wild and wonderful designs typical of Eastern ethnic traditions along with traditional Western fit. The pattern begins on the toe-sole; the toe then wraps around to the top, where pattern starts at the tip.

There is an Eastern technique for casting on in two colors that fools the eye by appearing to align stitches that go in opposite directions. Created for use at the tip of the toe, the process is very clumsy. Not only that, the results are not highly satisfactory when worked over more than a few stitches.

Therefore, I choose the option of making the toe pattern different from the rest of the sole pattern. This allows me to cast on in one color, yet stay true to the basic concept of Eastern design. If these designs are appealing, you might want to refer to my *Ethnic Socks and Stockings* for further inspiration.

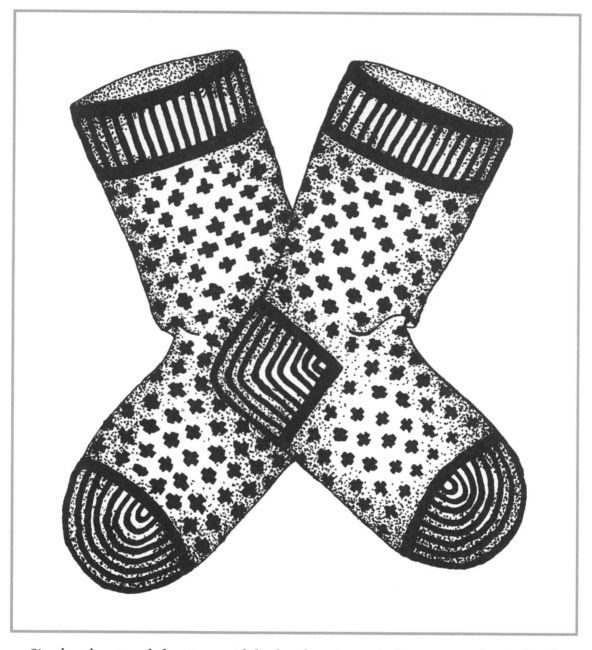

*Simple color-stranded pattern with heel and toe in vertical stripes, top finished with
vertical stripes and bound off with two ends of one color.*

Color patterns

Color-stranding

Color-stranded patterns are worked on this kind of sock just as they are on other socks. And they affect the elasticity in just the same way. As a general rule, the more colors per row and the longer the floats, the less the elasticity. If you have a problem adjusting tension to maintain elasticity, I suggest that you work color-stranded rows on needles one size larger than those you use for solid-color rows. The difference in gauge between these rows does not cause a problem. Since the pattern does affect elasticity, always work a circular gauge swatch to be sure that my sock will fit properly.

Handling multiple colors of yarns and securing floats

You have three choices for holding the yarns when working in two colors: one color in the left hand and one color in the right hand; two colors in the left hand; two colors in the right hand. All three of the options are good and relatively simple. I used to prefer carrying in both hands when working color patterns, but my left hand no longer works as it should so I now carry two colors in the right hand.

With two colors, one in each hand, I carry the dominant color to the right. The stitches are then knitted according to the design, both from the right and from the left.

When the dominant color is in the right hand, it is easy to secure long floats when they occur in the secondary color (left hand). Just lift the left finger to raise the floating yarn and cross with the main-color yarn to work the next stitch. When the left finger is lowered, the main color will again cross over to secure the floating color. When feasible, I like to work a second stitch before lowering the yarn to recross it, thus reducing the possibility that the floating color will peek through the stitches.

When it becomes necessary to secure a float in the main-color yarn (right hand), I usually use the "wrap, wrap, unwrap" technique when knitting socks. After entering the stitch, "wrap" the floating right yarn around the needle tip; "wrap" the left yarn (the color used in the new stitch now being worked) around the needle tip; then "unwrap" the floating yarn to take it back into position before drawing the new stitch (left-hand yarn) through the loop of the former row. Again, when feasible, I repeat this maneuver a second time to limit the possibility that the float yarn will peek through.

I seldom carry two colors in my left hand these days. But when I do, I carry one yarn on each side of my index finger. When one of the color floats needs to be secured to the back, I snake the needle tip around the float to bring the working color into position to cross the floating yarn.

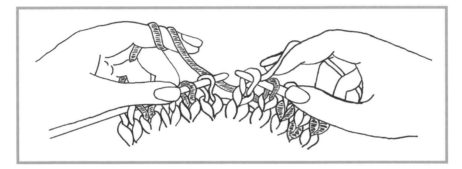

Carrying one color in each hand.

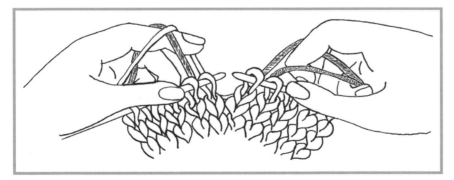

Carrying two colors in each hand.
When two colors are carried in only one hand, select the right or left version shown.

Most of the time I carry two colors in the right hand, again with one color on each side of my index finger. With the yarns in this position, the yarn on top of the finger is lifted to knit while the yarn on the underside of the finger is scooped up to knit. To secure a float, the positions of the two yarns are reversed. If the yarns are reversed alternately, top-to-bottom and then bottom-to-top, the two yarns do not become twisted.

A final note on securing the floating yarn: whenever possible, regardless of how you carry your yarn, secure the float behind a stitch of the same color. Then any color that shows through will match that of the surface stitch. If the main color is light, try to secure the floats behind darker contrasting colors, to minimize the possibility that color will show through to the surface.

With practice, you can learn to carry four colors with relative ease. When I need a fifth color, I let that color hang free, manipulating it with my right second finger as necessary. I seldom work with more than three colors any more (two in my right hand, one in my left hand); three gives me the ability to outline and highlight a design, which is sufficient for my needs.

An Afghani two-color bind-off technique

Borrowing from the design traditions of Afghanistan, try binding off in two colors for a nice finishing touch on color-stranded socks. The bind-off corners around the upper edge. The bound-off heads lie on the face and the twisted floats lie across the top.

Knit the first stitch in one color, bringing the contrasting color from underneath to twist. Knit the next stitch in the contrasting color, then pass the first stitch over it. Continue binding off in the alternating colors, always bringing the new yarn from underneath the old to twist.

This edging resists rolling, eliminating the need for a ribbing with color-stranded patterns. When working with a solid color in stockinette, I usually work one round in purl immediately before the two-color bind-off, to insure resistance to rolling. This bind-off is equally nice worked with two ends of one color. Take care to bind off somewhat loosely to avoid a tight, restrictive edging on the sock.

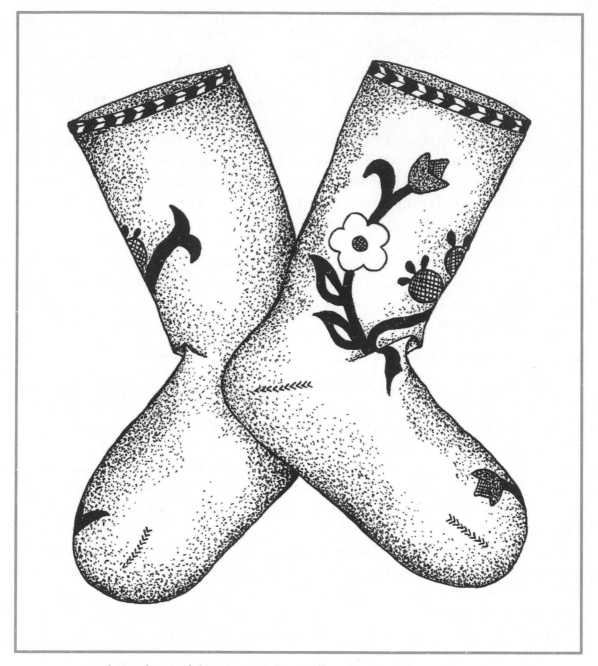

Socks with motif design, with bind-off worked in alternating colors.

Motif knitting

A motif is a design that does not require the yarn to be carried around the entire circumference of the work; it is a modified form of intarsia that appears to have evolved in Bulgaria. This type of design can be quite complex, but some background stitches (in the main color) must be incorporated into the design. The pattern is worked in a repetition of two rounds as follows.

1 *Color-stranded row:* The design is color-stranded in the pattern color/colors and the main color. When you reach the left side of the motif, drop the pattern color/colors. Continue knitting in the main color around the sock.

2 *Two-step row:*

(a) The main-color yarn is now at the right edge of the motif. Continue to knit across the motif, knitting all the main-color stitches in the motif while slipping as if to purl all the stitches that require the pattern color/colors. Drop the main-color yarn at the left side of the motif.

(b) Beginning at the left edge of the motif, knit in reverse (see next page) or turn the work to purl back across the motif. On this pass, all the stitches in the pattern color/colors are worked while all the main-color stitches (worked on the first pass) are slipped as if to purl. The pattern color/colors are picked up so they come up and over (cross) the main-color yarn.

When you reach the right edge of the motif again, drop the pattern color/colors, which will be in position to knit the next color-stranded row.

Return to the left edge of the motif and continue work with the main color to complete the round. You will be back at the right edge of the motif, with all colors ready for step 1, the color-stranded row.

Repeat steps 1 & 2 until the motif is complete.

Knitting in reverse

Knitting in reverse (i.e., backward) keeps the motif pattern on the side of the fabric that is facing you as you work. To create a standard knit stitch in reverse, working from left to right, enter the stitch with the left needle tip from left to right, behind the right needle tip. Wrap the yarn from back to front, coming up and over the left needle tip. Draw the yarn wrap through the loop on the right needle to form the new stitch on the left needle.

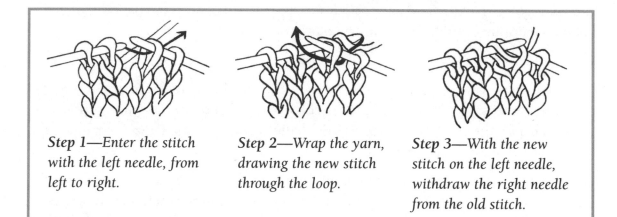

Step 1—Enter the stitch with the left needle, from left to right.

Step 2—Wrap the yarn, drawing the new stitch through the loop.

Step 3—With the new stitch on the left needle, withdraw the right needle from the old stitch.

Knitting in reverse, standard knit stitch.

Zigzag intarsia

Again in this technique, the pattern color does not encircle the sock. The section can be as little as one stitch but should not be more than a few stitches (up to one inch maximum). I find this technique most useful for a narrow, vertical stripe.

On the first round, the pattern color is stranded with the main color, and the main-color float is woven behind every stitch of the pattern color. The pattern color is dropped to the left, and the main color continues to the end of the round. When the pattern section is reached, the pattern color at the left is brought across the back to the right, twisted with the main-color yarn, and the row is worked as before.

True intarsia

Once again, the colors of the design do not encircle the sock. Instead, there are blocks of color that must be knitted flat. There are a number of ways to work intarsia "seamless," but all depend upon working flat rows back and forth, with the ends of the rows interlocked in some manner.

Yarn-over decrease technique

For socks, I find a flat row made into a circle with a yarn-over decrease technique the most sensible true-intarsia option, because it allows me to move from circular knitting to flat knitting and back to circular knitting with ease. The vertical join becomes the seamline.

Each section of the design requires a separate color bobbin (or center-pull butterfly). Starting at the seamline, yarn-over and knit with color 1 to the first color change. Drop color 1. Reach under to bring up the yarn of color 2 (twisting the yarns), and knit with color 2. Drop color 2. Reach under to bring up color 3 (twisting the yarns), and knit color 3.

Continue in this manner around the circumference of the sock, working up to the last stitch of the row. Complete the round with an SSK decrease, joining the yarn-over from the beginning of the row with the last stitch. Turn.

Yarn-over and purl, twisting the yarns as before at each color change. Purl up to the last stitch of the row. Complete the round with a P2tog, joining the yarn-over at the beginning of the row with the last stitch.

Knitting-in-reverse technique

True intarsia can also be worked by knitting in reverse as described on the previous page, with the design always facing forward. When you work in this manner, the last stitch is joined with the yarn-over with a K2tog.

South American intarsia technique

Another technique for working true intarsia has its roots in Andean knitting, specifically in the socks of Bolivia and Ecuador. With this technique, there is *no* visible join, because the connecting points for the rows follow the path of one of the color changes. Although entire socks can be worked in this manner (yes, argyles!), I find this method particularly useful for cuffs. As in the yarn-over decrease technique, the tube is worked back and forth in knit and purl rows, not in circular rounds, and instead of purling you can knit in reverse if you like. This technique is not difficult, although it is confusing on the first attempt.

To begin, knit the first round of the intarsia design in the standard manner for the tube, twisting the colors as usual at each color change. When you finish this round, continue the work *in rows* throughout the design portion.

Step-by-step, the process is as follows:

1   Turn the work so that the purl side faces you. When you do this, the yarns will all be at the right edges of their color sections, in working position.

2   As you begin the row, twist the yarn of the first color section and the yarn of what will become the last color section for this row. This sets you up to make the join at the end of the row, the "seamless" part of this technique. The yarn for the first color section is where it needs to be, at the right edge of its area. Yet the yarn for the last color section in the row is also at the right edge of its area, which is not where it apparently needs to be in order to be part of this twist. Twist these two yarns together anyway, allowing the yarn of the last color section to float across the face of the stitches to the twisting point. Don't worry about the float. It will disappear at the end of the row. You are now ready to begin purling.

3   As you purl the row, twist the yarns at each color change in the standard manner, by bringing the new color under the old, then dropping the old section's color and continuing with the color of the new section.

4   At the last color section, the final yarn does not appear to be available for use because it is secured at both ends. Instead, you have a float that originates in the stitches of the previous row at the color change and travels across the section before

Steps 2 & 3—*You will purl the first row from right to left. Begin by twisting the yarn of the first section together with what will become the yarn of the last section. Work the row as usual, twisting together the old and new colors at each change point.*

Step 4—*When you reach the final color change of the row, slip the yarn being dropped through the loop that crosses the final section. This produces a standard twist at the last color-change point.*

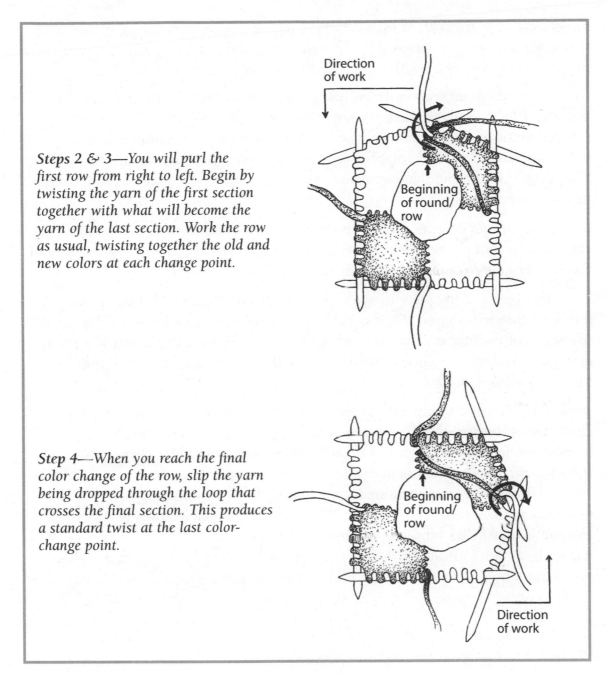

Invisible-join intarsia, *steps 2 through 4.*

being secured in the twist at the start of the row. In the next step, we will deal with this. For now, twist the yarns of the second-to-last and last sections by slipping the yarn of the second-to-last color through the floating loop of the last color.

5 To work the final section, create a working length of yarn with which to knit by pulling on the float of the last color. The yarn slides easily through the twist that secures it to the beginning of the row. Pull the looped yarn until enough of it is free for you to knit comfortably, even though the far end is not completely loose. Beginning with the end that comes out of the last stitch of the previous row, work this final section.

6 At the turning point of the beginning of the row, eliminate what remains of the yarn loop by pulling the excess back through the twist. The first and last sections of this row have been seamlessly joined, and the piece is again circular.

7 When you turn the piece to work in the other direction, continuing in rows rather than rounds, repeat this process of setting up the end of the row by twisting the colors of the first and last sections right at the start. Note that when you change directions, you will be working with different "first" and "last" colors—the color that was first is now last.

That is the basic technique. Yet when working intarsia with an invisible join, you must also be able to shift the starting points of your rows according to the design, because the join always occurs at a color change. When the color change shifts to the left, you can work across to the new starting point *or* you can slip stitches from left to right at the end of the round until you reach the new starting point, thus maintaining the integrity of each row. When the color change moves to the right, you can leave stitches unworked at the end of the row (and begin the new row where the design indicates it should start) or you can complete the row and then slip stitches from right to left to go back to the new starting point, again maintaining the integrity of the row.

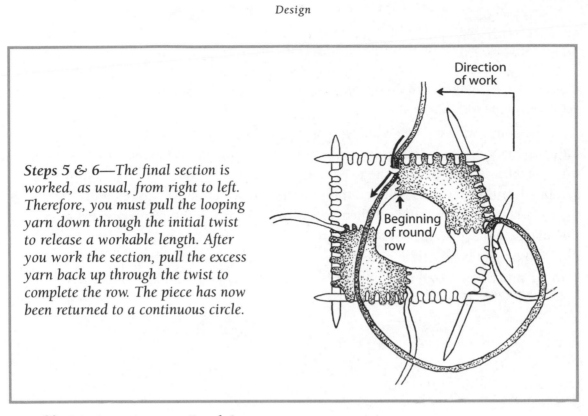

Steps 5 & 6—The final section is worked, as usual, from right to left. Therefore, you must pull the looping yarn down through the initial twist to release a workable length. After you work the section, pull the excess yarn back up through the twist to complete the row. The piece has now been returned to a continuous circle.

Direction of work

Beginning of round/ row

Invisible-join intarsia, steps 5 and 6.

In most cases, I prefer to maintain the integrity of each row, particularly when I work a detailed design with a lot of color shifts or when the shift occurs over a goodly number of stitches. But if I were working argyles, I would use the other technique because the color changes only shift by one stitch at a time in either direction.

If you use the method for maintaining the integrity of each row, the yarn will float across the back of the piece where you have slipped stitches to reach the new starting point. If this float is long, secure it on the following row by taking the needle tip under the float before working a stitch. Work the stitch and then draw the needle tip back under the float. When you work the following stitch, the working yarn will cross over the float and secure it.

*If your gauge changes when you shift
between round and flat knitting*

Your gauge may change when you shift from knitting the sock in the round to knitting the motif flat. If the change is significant, you should consider adapting the way the yarn is wrapped on the needle when you make a purl or reverse-knit stitch. Wrapped in the standard manner, the purl/reverse-knit stitch requires more yarn than the standard knit stitch. When you wrap the yarn in the non-standard manner, the disparity disappears. But the new stitch will be mounted with the leading side of the loop on the back of the needle. Thus, on the next row, stitches wrapped in this manner must be knitted through the back loop to make a standard knit stitch.

Adapted wrap for purl stitch

Wrapping purl stitch, coming over the needle tip from back to front, making the new stitch with the leading side of its loop on the back of the needle.

Adapted wrap for reverse-knit stitch

Wrapping the reverse-knit stitch, coming over the needle tip from front to back, making the new stitch with the leading side of its loop on the back of the needle.

Knitting adapted wrap stitches on the next row

New stitch, knitted through the back loop with a standard wrap.

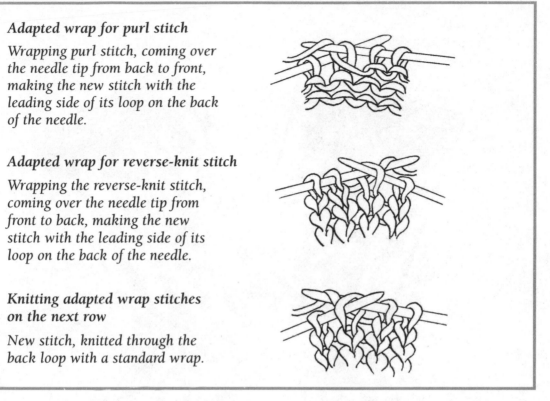

Purl/reverse-knit stitch with non-standard stitch mount.

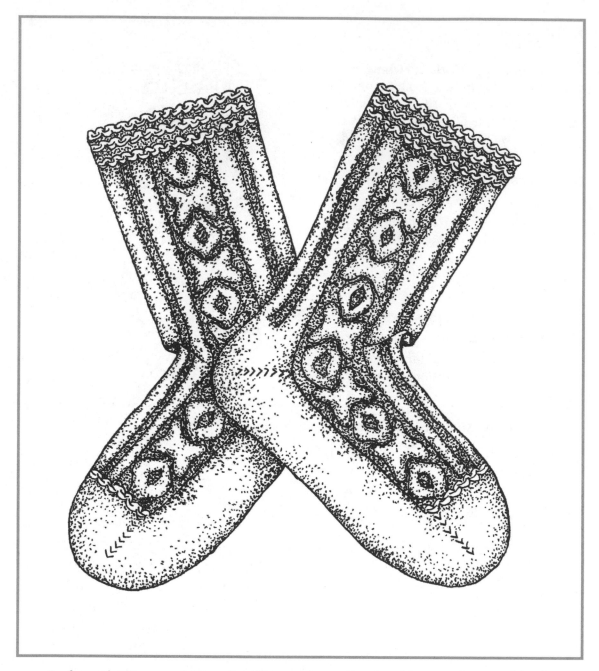

Socks with "Hugs and Kisses" cable at sides and wide ribbing at front and back.

Texture patterns

Texture patterns reduce elasticity, whether they are sculptured patterns with groups of stitches crossing over other groups of stitches, or traveling stitch patterns with one or two stitches moving left or right over the ground stitches. You must work your gauge swatch in the chosen pattern in the round to determine gauge. With enough experience, you will learn to guesstimate how many additional stitches may be required to make a sock—but be prepared for errors!

Sculptured patterns

These patterns require the use of a cable needle. When stitches are moved to the RIGHT in front of other stitches, the back stitches are placed on a cable needle at the BACK to be worked after the front stitches are completed. When stitches are moved to the LEFT in front of other stitches, the front stitches are placed on the cable needle at the FRONT to be worked after the stitches on the back.

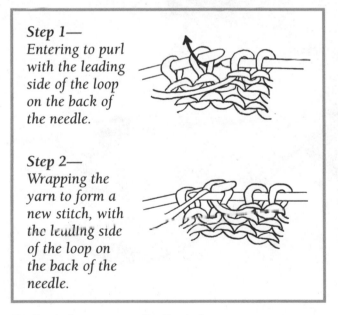

Step 1—Entering to purl with the leading side of the loop on the back of the needle.

Step 2—Wrapping the yarn to form a new stitch, with the leading side of the loop on the back of the needle.

Purl stitch, non-standard stitch mount.

Some knitters have a problem with loose edge stitches on cabled patterns. If this happens, the solution again lies in adapting the manner in which the purl stitches are wrapped. A standard purl stitch requires more yarn in the wrap than does a standard knit stitch. To eliminate the disparity, the yarn should be wrapped over the needle tip from back to front. The resulting stitch will have the leading side of the loop on the back of the needle and must be worked through the back of the loop on the next round.

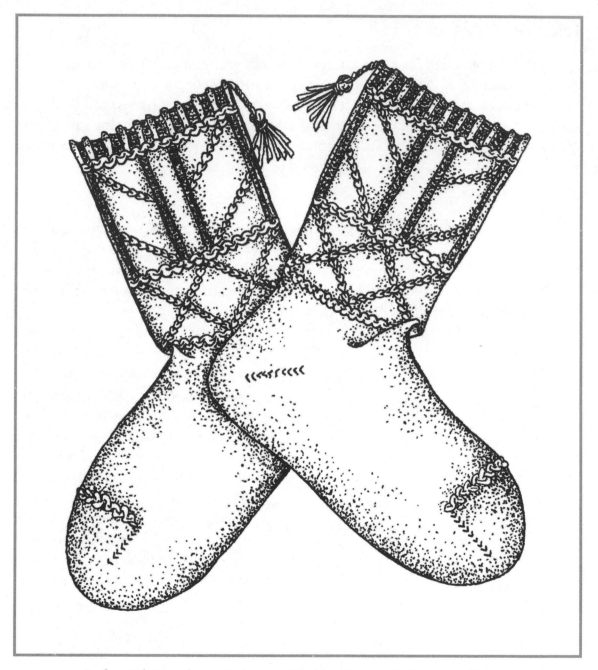

Socks with traveling stitches inspired by Eastern knitting traditions.

Traveling stitches

Traveling stitches are knit stitches that move left or right over the surface of the fabric, changing position on every row. This is, ideally, a circular technique that probably originated in sock knitting. Stitches are usually worked singly or in groups of two and do not require the use of a cable needle. In European knitting, the knit stitches are twisted and travel over a purl ground. In Eastern ethnic knitting, the knit stitches are not twisted and most often travel over a knit ground.

In either case, the stitches can be worked out of order (going beyond the first stitch to work the second stitch, then working the second stitch before moving any of the stitches to the right needle). Or the order can be changed before working the stitches. I now work only in the latter method, because it is easier on my hands. Written instructions for this method are on pages 87 and 88, and drawings appear on page 89.

Moving the SECOND *stitch on the left needle*
to the RIGHT *in front of the first stitch*

To change the order of the stitches, move the second stitch on the left needle to the *right* in front of the first stitch:

1 Take the right needle tip in front of the first stitch and enter the second stitch as if to purl.

2 Remove both stitches from the left needle, freeing the first stitch.

3 Take the left needle tip across the back to enter the free stitch from left to right.

4 Bring the second stitch (now on the right needle) across the front of the first stitch, and place it on the left needle tip. The two stitches are now ready to work in the new order. They can be twisted by knitting through the back loop in the traditional European manner or left untwisted in the Eastern manner.

*Moving the FIRST stitch on the left needle
to the LEFT in front of the second stitch*

To change the order of the stitches, move the first stitch on the left needle to the *left* in front of the second stitch:

1 Take the right needle tip behind the first stitch and enter the second stitch as if to purl.

2 Remove the left needle from both stitches, freeing the first stitch.

3 Take the left needle tip across the front to enter the free stitch from left to right.

4 Place the second stitch (now on the right needle) onto the left needle. The two stitches are now ready to work in the new order. As before, they can be twisted by knitting through the back loop in the traditional European manner or left untwisted in the Eastern manner.

If you decide to knit your traveling stitches through the back loop....

When the knit stitches are twisted, they are tightened and become more distinct, especially on a purl ground. Traditionally, the knit stitches are twisted by knitting through the back loop of a standard stitch mount. This results in a crossed knit stitch that leans to the left. I like to make all crossed stitches traveling to the left (or in the left half of a repeat) in this manner. However, I make my crossed knit stitches traveling to the right (or in the right half of a repeat) lean to the right by adjusting the stitch mount. I place the leading side of the loop on the back (non-standard stitch mount) and knit through the front loop (the trailing side of the loop). This results in a crossed knit stitch leaning to the right.

Although I use traditional alpine patterns, I like the symmetry provided by adapting the directional cross of each traveling stitch.

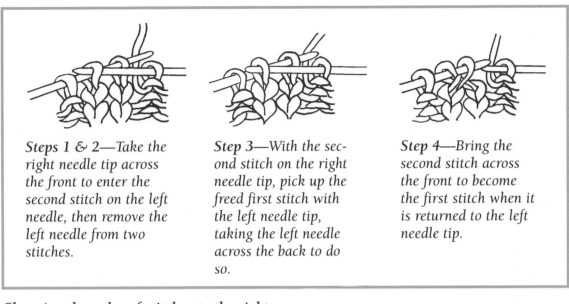

Steps 1 & 2—*Take the right needle tip across the front to enter the second stitch on the left needle, then remove the left needle from two stitches.*

Step 3—*With the second stitch on the right needle tip, pick up the freed first stitch with the left needle tip, taking the left needle across the back to do so.*

Step 4—*Bring the second stitch across the front to become the first stitch when it is returned to the left needle tip.*

Changing the order of stitches to the right.

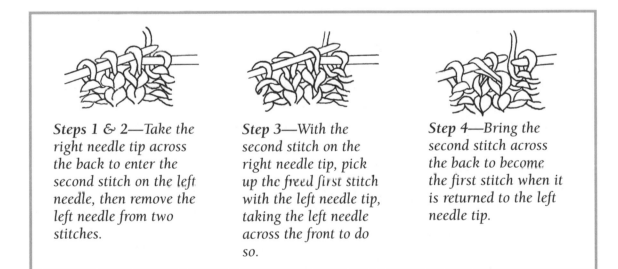

Steps 1 & 2—*Take the right needle tip across the back to enter the second stitch on the left needle, then remove the left needle from two stitches.*

Step 3—*With the second stitch on the right needle tip, pick up the freed first stitch with the left needle tip, taking the left needle across the front to do so.*

Step 4—*Bring the second stitch across the back to become the first stitch when it is returned to the left needle tip.*

Changing the order of stitches to the left.

Lace patterns

Carefully select your yarn for lace patterns, because the yarn is more important than the pattern itself. A smooth, round, combed or worsted yarn with a fair amount of twist is necessary to show the pattern clearly. Clarity of pattern results in greater beauty than intricacy of design.

As with all design elements, lace patterns alter gauge. In the case of lace, you will need to use fewer circumference stitches so that the the open work will stretch sufficiently to show the pattern. As usual, there is no shortcut for working a gauge swatch in pattern. Unless you have knitted a lot of lace socks, guesstimating usually leads to disappointment.

The drawing on the opposite page represents the socks that led me to the short-row technique for heel and toe. The pattern is this: (YO, K2tog) 3 times on first round, knit second round. Repeat these two rounds, with the pattern in vertical orientation. Simple, but so elegant when worked at 12 stitches per inch in the crisp cotton/linen yarn of the original pair.

Correcting errors

All of us make mistakes. In color work, they are easy to spot and correct on the next row. This is not always the case when working texture or lace patterns in a single color. And with stitches changing order, decreasing and increasing with yarn-overs, and other intricate maneuvers, fixing these errors can seem traumatic.

This need not be the case. I keep short, double-pointed "finger" needles at hand, preferably a size or two smaller than the needles used in the project. Instead of trying to work down one stitch at a time to the error, I pull out all the stitches of the horizontal repeat within which the error has occurred, down to and including the row with the error. For a six-stitch pattern, I therefore "unknit" only the six stitches of the one repeat that contains the error. This leaves a strand of yarn floating across the back for every row I have unknitted. Using the smaller, short needles, I pick up the live stitches at the base of the unknitted area—in this case, the six stitches of that repeat—and begin to re-knit those six stitches, using the first floating strand of yarn across the back. With the right side of the fabric facing me, I knit

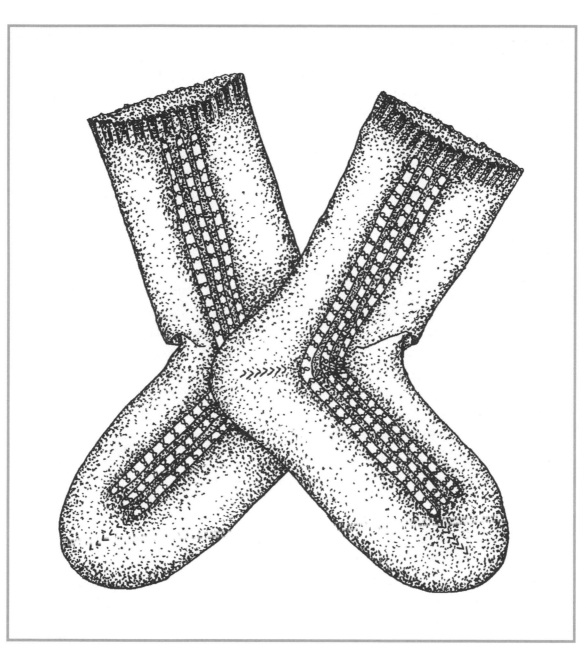

Socks with simple lace pattern.
See my comments (opposite page) on where a pair of socks like this led me.

the appropriate row of the pattern. If the repeat includes more than three or four stitches, I manipulate the yarn with my right hand for the first half and with my left hand for the second half; this helps to even the tension on the stitches from side to side. I continue in this manner, always with the right side facing me, working each row with its own floating strand. I then continue where I left off.

This is much easier than pulling out several rounds—and not the least bit frustrating.

Adapting size to design

The chosen stitch pattern will not always fit neatly with the required stitch and row counts of the sock. The horizontal stitch repeat may require too few or too many stitches, or the vertical row repeat may require too few or too many rows to coincide perfectly with the sock dimensions. Fortunately, the flexibility of knit fabric can help you make socks that fit and accommodate a specific pattern repeat.

If the closest multiple of your stitch repeat makes a sock that is slightly too wide, reduce the length a bit. Conversely, if the closest multiple makes a sock that is slightly too narrow, increase the length slightly to compensate.

The same holds true in the other direction. If your row repeat makes a sock that is a little too short, increase the width a bit. If the row repeat makes a sock that is slightly too long, decrease the width.

You can also apply this fudge factor when your sock gauge does not perfectly match your swatch gauge, in lieu of ripping out and starting over. Ah yes, one of the beauties of hand-knit socks is their willingness to compromise!

Postscript

Short-row socks are great fun to knit and a greater pleasure to wear because they are so easily custom fitted to the individual foot. Whether plain or fancy, these simple socks offer one of the greater pleasures of being a hand knitter—NIRVANA!

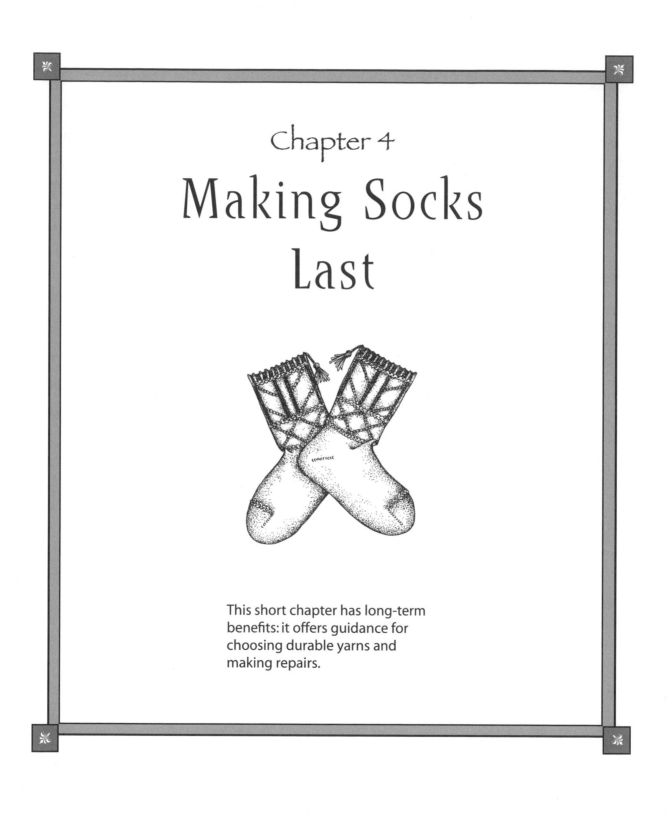

Chapter 4
Making Socks Last

This short chapter has long-term
benefits: it offers guidance for
choosing durable yarns and
making repairs.

Socks are exposed to harsh conditions, including heat, moisture, and abrasion when on the foot and in a shoe. Even greater abrasion and snagging await the bare sock. Thus socks are worn out more quickly than other garments.

The greatest extenders of life are the careful selection of the yarn and a firm knitting gauge. Yet the short-row sock structure also lends itself beautifully to replacement of the areas most likely to wear through: heels and toes.

Fibers

Wool, cotton, linen, and silk are all traditional fibers used in knitting socks. Wool and cotton are most often used today, in addition to the synthetic fibers. Synthetic fibers are the most durable, but 100% synthetic yarns are not very comfortable to wear. Synthetics are not absorbent and become clammy when used for socks. In blends with the natural fibers, synthetics extend the life of the yarn without becoming unpleasant to wear. Nylon is most often used in blends with wool and cotton.

Nylon is also used to make reinforcement yarns for the heel and toe. It has been my experience (and that of many others) that reinforcement yarns actually cut the natural-fiber yarns instead of making them more durable. But reinforcement yarns make a nice mesh on which to do duplicate stitch when the sock yarn wears out. This looks as good as most darning, better than some.

I prefer to work with wool and cotton.

I like 100% wool, and as a handspinner, I can select the softer longwool fibers that are incredibly durable for my sock yarns. A wool-and-mohair blend is delightful. This incorporation of mohair expands the range of suitable wools for socks. Even by adding a bit of mohair to the heel and toe yarns, handspinners can make suitably durable socks from wools that would not otherwise wear well enough.

I am not particularly fond of 100% cotton for socks. It often looks and feels too much like string. Adding a small percentage of wool to cotton makes a delightful sock yarn. The wool increases elasticity and loft, making the yarn very comfortable—even for use in a summer sock, because the wool is highly absorbent.

When looking for a sock yarn, check the twist. A well-twisted, dense yarn will be much more durable than a soft, lofty yarn. Among the blends, look for those with more natural-fiber than synthetic-fiber content.

Repairs

One of the beauties of the simple sock structure is how simply it can be repaired. Either heel or toe can be replaced as a unit. A typical Western-style sock has the foot stitches picked up along the side of the heel-back; this makes removal very difficult. On the short-row sock, the heel can be removed easily because the shaping stitches are not connected to the stitches of the ankle or foot. Once the old heel has been removed, pick up across one portion of the circumference and knit the new heel. After you complete the heel, graft the new heel stitches to the other portion of the circumference stitches. You may need to apply the fudge factor at the two corners, but you have the yarn tails to take care of that small problem. And the socks will not look patched.

The toe is even easier to replace, especially if the sock was knitted top-to-toe. Pull out the toe and knit in a new one, just like the earlier toe. If the sock was knitted toe-to-top, you will have to clip a yarn and pick out one round stitch by stitch, then put the open stitches from the foot on two needles as usual and knit the new toe in place.

The leg of a sock lasts a long time if the cast-on or bind-off at its upper edge is sufficiently elastic. The cast-on and graft-off I recommend for the simple sock are very durable, and can be made more so if working with finer yarns. Work either technique with a double yarn—this both extends the lifespan of the sock and adds a slight decorative touch. And don't forget that you can easily replace the entire foot, reusing just the leg of the sock!

Chapter 5
Beyond Socks
to Mittens

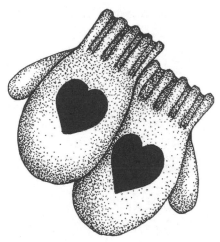

Once you're familiar with short-row shaping in socks, take the technique further: to the hands and thumbs of mittens.

- Consider starting your mittens from their tips.

- A bit of short-row work across the back of the hand produces mittens that both feel and move better.

- Check out the thumb-shaping and placement options....

The first time you knit a pair of short-row socks, toe-to-top, your thoughts will likely turn to mittens. Yes, the sock toe is identical to a mitten tip. And mittens are best worked tip-to-top because the length is so easy to fit this way. But if you prefer to work top-to-tip, plan to graft the stitches on the palm side of the mitten.

Measurements

To fit the mitten, measure the widest part of the hand, adding about 10% for ease. You might be surprised to find that the hand is about 10% smaller in circumference than the foot. Yes, that means that you could use the same circumference measurement for both hand and foot, another one of those interesting body proportions. As with the foot, decide if the hand is pointed, average, or blunt to determine how many stitches must remain between the yarn-overs (stitches between yarn-overs = 15%/20%/25% of C).

Measurements for mitten-making

Mitten circumference in inches: C = widest part of hand plus 10% (approximately the same as foot circumference)

Length of hand: from longest fingertip to base of wrist-bone protrusion, minus 10%

Position of thumb: from longest fingertip to base of V at crotch of thumb, minus 10%

Length of thumb: from tip of thumb to base of V at crotch of thumb, minus 10%

❦

Stitches to cast on = C times gauge

Stitches between yarn-overs = 15%/20%/25% of C, depending on whether the hand is pointed, average, or blunt

---

Measure the total length of the hand from the tip of the longest finger to the base of the wrist-bone protrusion and decrease by 10%. To locate the position of the thumb on the mitten, measure from the tip of the longest finger to the base of the V in the crotch of the thumb and decrease by 10%. The thumb is located about two-thirds of the way up from the tip (66% of the total length). Measure the length of the thumb from its tip to the base of the V, again decreasing by 10%.

Choices for how to make and shape mittens

I start my mittens at the tip, working up to the cuff. The tip of the mitten is worked just like the tip of the toe, using the invisible cast-on on the palm side of the mitten. You can chose to work from the cuff down, locating the thumb one-third of the way down from the base of the cuff (33% of the length). But working from the cuff down requires that you graft the tip-stitches to the palm stitches to complete the mitten. And the Vs of the knit stitches will be standing on their heads, a personal hangup for me!

After completing the tip, I like to shape the mitten so it curves to fit my hand when relaxed. When I do this, the mittens fit better and do not bunch up when the hand grasps something. Yes, short-row shaping is the answer, worked so there are more rows on the back of the mitten hand than on its palm. The technique varies slightly from the yarn-over technique previously described, because these short rows must blend into flat rounds, not turn a corner. The short-row variation for mittens is described in detail on pages 104–06. (This version of the short-row technique is also excellent for shaping the back of a circular yoke sweater so that it fits the contours of the body better.)

Because I knit the hand from the tip up, I also begin the thumb at its tip. The thumb circumference is one-third of the hand circumference (33% of C), yet another interesting proportion. The tip of the thumb can begin with the same short-row technique as the tip of the hand or with a circular cast-on. When you work the short-row technique, leave two or three stitches between the yarn-overs at the tip. And when you join the thumb to the hand, be sure that its shaping parallels the shaping at the tip of the hand.

A circular cast-on

When I work with a circular cast-on, I use a modification of the old German circular cast-on (often referred to as the Emily Ocker circular cast-on). The traditional way uses a crochet hook to pick up the stitches. I prefer to work this type of cast-on with a knitting needle instead, thus eliminating both the round of crochet heads and the transfer of stitches from hook to knitting needle.

For this version, make a nickel-sized circle of yarn, leaving a tail with which to close up the small circular opening after you have knitted a few rounds. With a knitting needle, draw a loop up through the center of the circle. Snug this first stitch securely on the needle. Then draw a second loop up from the outside of the circle; pull the third loop from the inside, the fourth from the outside, the fifth from the inside. Continue in this manner until you have the number of stitches that you need. I usually pick up half the number of stitches that are really required for the thumb circumference, knit one round to divide the stitches on the needles, then repeat "knit one/make-one raised" around to reach the full number. If you need an odd number of stitches, the last stitch comes from the inside of the circle; if you need an even number of stitches, the last stitch comes from the outside of the circle and looks like a yarn-over.

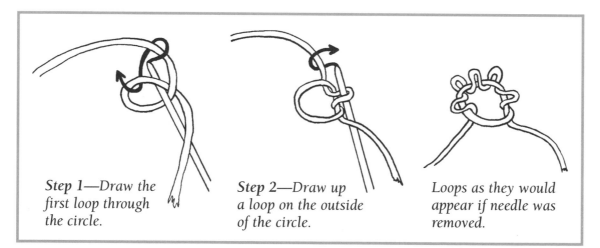

Step 1—Draw the first loop through the circle.

Step 2—Draw up a loop on the outside of the circle.

Loops as they would appear if needle was removed.

Circular cast-on for thumb.

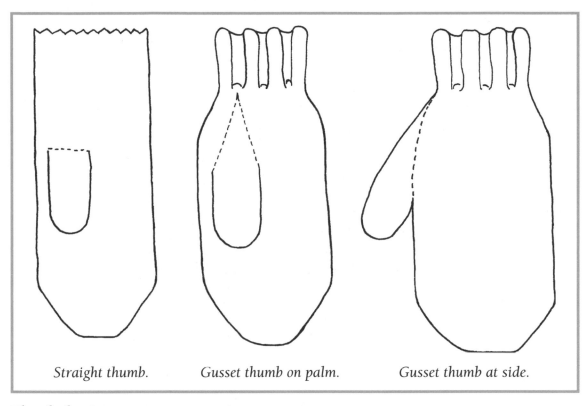

Straight thumb.   *Gusset thumb on palm.*   *Gusset thumb at side.*

Thumb shapings.

Shaping and placing the thumbs

I use two thumb shapings: a straight thumb on the palm and a gusset thumb on the palm or at the side. Either of these thumbs can be attached to the hand on the palm, so the mittens become right- and left-handed. The gusset thumb can also be attached at the side to produce mittens that can be swapped between the hands, if the patterning permits. The gusset structure conforms more readily to the hand, thus it is usually considered to be the more comfortable style. The straight thumb is the easiest to make but, unless very generously fitted, does not conform to the hand as well as a thumb with a gusset. Yet when you want to match patterns across the thumb and the palm of the mitten, the straight thumb is usually a better choice.

For a right- and left-hand mitten, the thumb is usually inset a few stitches from the edge of the palm, although some knitters prefer to place it at the edge. I usually inset the thumb by the number of stitches equal to about 5% of C. For interchangeable mittens, half the thumb stitches are positioned on the back of the mitten hand and half on its palm.

To attach the thumb, half the thumb circumference stitches are joined to an equal number of stitches on the mitten hand, while the remaining half replace the stitches just removed from the mitten hand to become a part of the circumference. The stitches can be bound off together or grafted. I prefer to graft the stitches, because the join is more flexible. But grafting the stitches can leave a gap at each end. To close the gap, I pick up a stitch at each end of the grafting row, then remove it almost immediately—when I work the first round after the join—by using the appropriate decrease (a K2tog on the right side and an SSK on the left side).

The straight thumb requires no further shaping. Just knit a wrist section and the cuff on the number of stitches established for the circumference.

The base of the gusset thumb does need to be shaped. When placed on the palm (assuming that you are working from the tip), the gusset thumb stitches are decreased by one on each side—consumed by a palm stitch with an SSK on the right side or a K2tog on the left on every third/fourth round—until all the thumb stitches have been removed. This narrows the mitten to conform to the wrist.

For a gusset thumb placed at the side, half the thumb stitches are joined to the mitten hand. In this case, the thumb is centered at the side, half of the stitches coming from the back of the mitten hand and half coming from its palm. As before, the stitches can be bound off together or grafted. And the thumb is decreased on each side on every third/fourth round.

When working from the cuff down, no shaping is necessary for the straight thumb. When you reach the thumb position, work a waste yarn across the required number of stitches (half of the thumb circumference). Then continue working the mitten hand to the tip. Then remove the waste yarn, pick up the stitches, and work the thumb down to its tip. Or you can place the stitches for half of the thumb circumference on a holder, and cast on an equal number as replacements on which you continue the mitten hand.

These options are easy, but I find it unpleasant to knit the thumb with the rest of the mitten hand dangling.

When working from the cuff down, the gusset thumb must be positioned at the beginning of the wrist, whether for the inset thumb on the palm or the thumb at the side. The shaping is then reversed from the tip-up structure, requiring increases on each side of the thumb on every third/fourth round. When half the thumb circumference stitches lie between the increase lines, these stitches are placed on hold and new stitches are cast on, with which you continue the hand of the mitten. After you finish the hand, pick up the thumb stitches and work the thumb down to the tip.

The cuff of a mitten is equivalent to the leg on a crew sock. As such, it is finished (or started) with the same techniques.

Step-by-step instructions for short-row shaping on the back of a mitten hand

1 Short rows begin four/six rounds after you complete the mitten tip. (Or, if you started at the cuff, four/six rows after the thumb line.) In addition, you will work the short rows themselves at four-round or six-round intervals; the four-round intervals produce greater curvature in the mitten than the six-round intervals do.

2 Knit across all stitches for the back of the hand. Turn.

3 Purl side facing, slip the first stitch as if to purl; work across all stitches for the back of the hand. Turn.

4 Knit side facing, slip the first stitch as if to purl. Do not snug the working yarn in tightly when crossing behind the slip stitch to work the following knit stitch. Work up to and including the slip stitch at the far side.

Step-by-step instructions for short-row shaping on the back of a mitten hand *(continued)*

5 *Short-row join, knit side facing, left side of short row:*

(a) Fold the work forward to expose its wrong side, and use the left needle tip to lift the bar that connects the slip stitch to the next stitch on the left needle. This bar, when lifted, tightens the slip stitch just worked.

(b) Lift the bar from top to bottom with the left needle tip, so the leading side of the bar loop is on the front of the needle.

(c) K2tog to join the slip stitch and the bar loop of the previous row.

Step 5a—Fold the work forward to see its back, lifting the bar that tightens the slip stitch.

Step 5b—K2tog, joining the next stitch with the bar loop.

How to complete the left side of a short row.

6 *Short-row join, knit side facing, right side of short row:*

(a) Knit around to the last stitch on the second palm needle, one stitch before the slip stitch on the first needle for the back of the hand. Slip this stitch to right needle as if to knit.

(b) Fold the work forward to expose its wrong side, and use the right needle tip to lift the bar that connects the slip stitch to the next stitch on the left

Step-by-step instructions for short-row shaping on the back of a mitten hand *(continued)*

needle. This bar comes directly out of the bottom of the slip stitch on the left needle. The slip stitch on the left needle and the bar loop on the right needle form a straight line when the needles are parallel to one another. The two loops will be tight. The bar loop must be lifted from bottom to top (so the leading side of the bar loop is on the back of the needle).

(c) Wrap the yarn around the right needle tip, then draw the yarn through the bar loop to create a new stitch on the right needle.

(d) With the left needle tip, pass the stitch that you slipped to the right needle a moment ago over the new stitch to join (PSSO decrease).

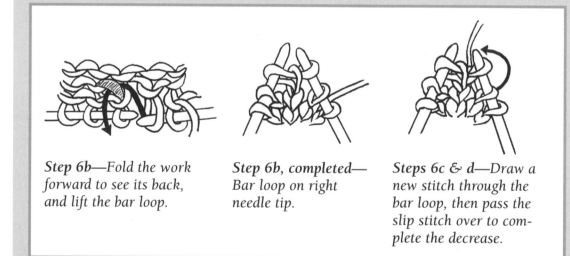

Step 6b—Fold the work forward to see its back, and lift the bar loop.

Step 6b, completed— Bar loop on right needle tip.

Steps 6c & d—Draw a new stitch through the bar loop, then pass the slip stitch over to complete the decrease.

How to complete the right side of a short row.

7 Knit four/six rounds, then repeat the short-row sequence (across and back) on the back of the hand. Continue in this manner until four/six rows before the thumb line. (Or, when working cuff-down, before the tip shaping.)

Designs on mittens

Designs are incorporated into the mitten just like the sock, unless you have shaped the mitten to fix the relaxed hand (pages 99 and 104–06). Patterns on the back of the hand are ideal for the relaxed mitten, especially motif patterns. Because the number of rows is different on the back of the hand and the palm, continuous color-stranded patterns are not suitable. But if the pattern is different on the back of the mitten and its palm, color-stranding can be adapted nicely to this mitten, especially if the designs are outlined. In this case, the palm pattern is usually a small, simple repeat while the back of the mitten hand will have a larger, more complex pattern. You must remember to adapt the pattern to accommodate the invisible cast-on, where the vertical lines are off by one-half stitch.

Postscript

Obviously, my passion lies with socks, but simple mittens by the short-row technique have much to offer to a knitter's repertoire.

❧

Notes for mitten-making

Recipient					
C (circumference)	inches				
L (length of hand)	inches				
Position of thumb	inches				
Length of thumb	inches				
Yarn					
Gauge	stitches/inch				
Needle size(s)					
Cast-on stitches					
Stitches between yarn-overs					

Notes for sock-making

Recipient					
C (circumference)	inches				
L (length)	inches				
Yarn					
Gauge	stitches/inch				
Needle size(s)					
Cast-on stitches					
Ankle rows					
Heel/toe stitches					
Stitches between yarn-overs					

Notes on measuring and body proportions

Basic measurement principles are on pages 18–20. Yet here is another fun set of proportions.

The circumference (C) of the fist, measured around the midpoint of the back of the hand, equals the circumference (C) of the foot at its widest part.

This measurement also corresponds to the total length of the foot (not the L of the book calculation, which is the total length minus the amount required for toe shaping) *and* to the total length of a mitten (when working tip-up, divide for thumb when half the length has been completed; when working from the cuff down, begin shaping the thumb when one-quarter of the length has been completed) *and* to the length of a crew sock's leg!

Traditional knitters developed their garments by understanding basic anatomical relationships of this sort, with the assistance of the wonderfully accommodating knitted structure.

. . . when finely crafted,
humble and elegant are equal. . . .

—Priscilla Gibson-Roberts

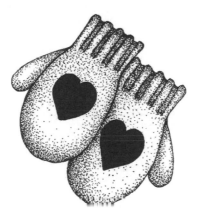

INDEX

A

Afghani two-color bind-off, 73, 74
Andean knitting, 78
ankle section, fitting, 19, 20, 21–22
arched feet, fitting adjustments, 19
argyle socks, 81
average fit, *see* fit/fitting

B

backward knitting, *see* reverse
    knitting
binding off
    Afghani two-color bind-off, 73,
        74
    needle size, 26
    top-to-toe construction, 38,
        43–45, 56
    zigzag bind-off, 38, 43, 56
    see also grafting off
blunt toes, fitting adjustments, 19,
    20
bull's-eye effect, 61–64

C

cable designs, 84, 85
carries
    for elastic cast-on, 32–35
    multiple colors, 71–73
casting on
    circular cast-on for mittens, 100
    for Eastern ethnic designs, 69
    needle size, 26
    toe-to-top construction, 46–47,
        56
    top-to-toe construction, 31–37
children's socks
    fitting chart, 23
    knee socks, 20
circular cast-on, 100
circular knitting
    dividing stitches on needles, 26,
        27, 31
    shifting to flat knitting, 77, 82

circumference
    mittens, 98
    socks, 18–20, 23–24
    with stockinette stitch, 54
color-stranding
    basic techniques, 71–73
    in motif knitting, 75
    for stripes, 64
    see also intarsia
colors
    changing colors, 67, 69
    contrasting colors at heel and
        toe, 60, 61
    handling multiple yarns, 71–73
commercial socks, as inspiration,
    14–15, 58
complex patterns, *see* design
    elements
Continental carry, 34–35
cotton, 95
counting stitches between yarn-
    overs, 20, 40, 49
crew socks
    increases/decreases for fancy
        socks, 58
    leg length, 108
    proportions, 20
    see also toe-to-top construction;
        top-to-toe construction
crossed stitches, 88
cuffs
    mittens, 104
    socks, 54, 55

D

Danish knitting, 63
darning, 14
    see also repairing socks
decreases
    back seams, 22, 58
    left-leaning, 30, 58
    reducing gaps, 47
    right-leaning, 31, 58

yarn-over technique, 77
design elements
    adapting size for, 92
    color, 60–61, 70–74
    ethnic patterns, 68, 69
    hems and cuffs, 54, 55
    intarsia, 76–81
    lace, 90–91
    for mittens, 107
    motifs, 74–76
    stripes, 61–67, 69
    texture, 84–88

E

Eastern-style socks
    adjusting fit, 21–22
    advantages of, 14
    ethnic designs, 68, 69
    increases/decreases for, 58
    joins, 27
    traveling stitches in, 87
    see also toe-to-top construction
elastic cast-ons, 32–35
elasticity, *see* gauge
Emily Ocker circular cast-on, 100
ends, working in, 53–54
English carry, 32–33
errors, correcting, 90, 92
ethnic designs, 68, 69
European knitting
    Continental carry, 34–35
    Danish knitting, 63
    German circular cast-on, 100
    old Norwegian sock cast-on,
        32–35
    traveling stitches in, 87
    see also Western-style socks

F

fancy patterns, *see* design elements
fiber types, 95–96
fit/fitting
    adapting for design elements, 92